ELLA

A Biography of Governor Ella Grasso

The

and Citizenship Education, Inc.

ELLA

A Biography of Governor Ella Grasso

Susan Bysiewicz

To SJB and SRB, JB and GB, KB and KB

Cover design by Frank Westerberg

Book design by Hildebrandt, Fisher Associates

Manufactured in the United States of America

ISBN 0-933614-24-1

"Politics is Property"

. . . Everybody in the game has a piece, and that piece is workable, it is equivalent to capital, it can be used to accrue interest by being invested in such sound conservative enterprises as decades of loyalty to the same Machine. So long as the system progresses, so will one's property be blessed by dividends.

Norman Mailer
Miami and the Siege of Chicago

Preface

Sitting at my desk in the Connecticut State Capitol, I look across my office to a table holding family photos and my children's artwork. This is the table on which Governor Ella T. Grasso lay in state as Connecticut residents lined up to pay their respects to "Mother Ella," the first woman elected governor in her own right in the nation. As a student at Yale, writing her biography in 1984, I could not foresee the day that I would be sitting in the Secretary of the State's Office, the same office held by Ella Grasso from 1959 to 1971 before she became Governor of Connecticut.

In my acknowledgements for the first printing in 1984, I wrote of my indebtedness to the many great women in Connecticut who inspired me to write this book. Today, I acknowledge them for the inspiration, not only to author a book, but also to run for public office myself. As an elected official, and a woman, I owe a debt of gratitude to women like Governor Grasso, who gave our state and nation an introduction to powerful women and turned the dream of attaining public office into a reality for so many other women leaders nationwide.

In Connecticut today, Ella Grasso's legacy is clear. Women serve at all levels of government – local, state and federal. Of the state's six constitutional offices, four are held by women in 2002. But we are still breaking barriers. I have been privileged to hold the office of Secretary of the State since 1999 and am the first Polish-American and Greek-American to be elected to statewide constitutional office in our state. My colleagues include State Treasurer Denise Nappier, the first woman to hold this office in Connecticut and the first African-American woman elected to the office of State Treasurer in the United States. Our State Comptroller, Nancy Wyman, is the first woman elected State Comptroller in Connecticut history. Jodi Rell has served as Connecticut's Lieutenant Governor since 1994. Moira Lyons is the first woman to serve as the Speaker of the House in our state and is currently one of only seven women nationally who serve as speakers or speakers pro tempore of a state house.

I believe that these "firsts" would not have been possible without Ella Grasso's trailblazing tenure as Governor and without the other women who have served our state and our country in elected office. I am gratified to know that young women can find role models in public service, and that they may consider a career in government as a way to contribute to their communities.

Although Connecticut is a national example for women at high levels of state government, only 27.6% of statewide offices across the country are held by women. In the 107th United States Congress, only 13.6% are women and, at the state level, 22.4% of state legislators are women. While women have been making strides at all levels of government we still have a long journey ahead of us to achieve parity in elected office. We need more women to make decisions which affect our daily lives, such as how to strengthen public education, expand health insurance coverage, and revitalize our economy. We need to be part of the discussion on taxes, transportation, and our environment. We must add our voices to discussions of national security, international trade and human rights.

As Connecticut Secretary of the State, one of my highest priorities has been motivating people to participate in our government. Whether through voting, volunteering on a local board or commission, or running for office, I have encouraged Connecticut residents to give back to their communities and to be active participants in our democracy.

In the not so distant past, women have traditionally chosen to contribute as volunteers, activists and in other capacities "outside" the traditional structures of government. Those times are changing. I am proud that my daughters will grow up to understand that it is natural for women to serve at all levels of government. Seeing is believing. By looking at Connecticut, every girl will know that she is capable of leading her city, her state or her nation. Thank you, Ella Grasso.

Susan Bysiewicz
Hartford, Connecticut
January, 2002

Acknowledgements

In the process of researching and writing this book, I have incurred many debts. Katherine McKula at the *Hartford Courant* library, Angel Diggs at the *New Haven Register* library, Theodore Wohlsen at the State Library, and Howard White at the Naughton Reed House gave me access to vital documents. Larrye deBear and John Purmont in the Governor's Office and Stephen Heinz in the Office of Policy Management also provided state documents and publications. Helen Loy at the University of Hartford and Attorney Amalia Toro, let me survey their personal collections of letters and photographs.

As I prepared to write, both Bernard Asbel, author of *The Senate Nobody Knows* and Joseph Lieberman, author of *The Power Broker*, urged me to simply "tell Ella's story." This proved to be the most important advice I received. Bruce Wessel and Michael Riley, both astute observers of state politics, proved invaluable in the beginning stages of this project.

Everybody knew Ella. I never had difficulty finding people to talk to me about her. Each person I spoke with, formally and informally, gave me useful insights. I thank the countless number of individuals I spoke with for sharing their time and perspectives, especially the Grasso family, Sylvio Preli, and Francis Draghi, who good naturedly answered my unceasing questions. I also want to express my appreciation to those who read through the many drafts of the manuscript. Cynthia Russett, Doug Yates, Lydia Tamez, Charles Berger, Mary Ramsbottom, Sylvio Preli, Francis Draghi, Bruce Wessel, and Gloria Duran, all demonstrated their stamina and goodwill throughout this project. Katherine Keenum deserves special thanks for her continuing patience and good spirits. In addition, I thank my editor, Barry Hildebrandt and his wife Susan for their generous assistance.

Like all major and minor endeavors in my family, this book was a group effort. My parents, my aunt Rose Bysiewicz, and my brother and sisters, John, Karen, and Gail, unselfishly acted as critics, proofreaders, and chauffeurs. My aunts, Mary Stewart, Evangeline Luddy, and Poppy Fowler survived the necessary technical and typing tasks.

Finally, I am indebted to many great women in Connecticut politics—Chase Going Woodhouse, Clair Booth Luce, Barbara Kennelly, Sara B. Crawford, Ann Ucello, Gloria Schaffer, Nancy Johnson, and Audrey Beck—who inspired me to write this book.

Susan Bysiewicz
West Berlin
January, 1984

Table of Contents

Chapter One

WINDSOR LOCKS
1919-1936

It was perhaps prophetic that the *Windsor Locks Journal* erred in its birth announcement of Ella Rosa Giovanna Tambussi. On May 16, 1919, the town weekly reported the birth of "a son to Mr. and Mrs. James Tambussi of Olive Street." No one at the time could have foreseen that a daughter, or for that matter a child of Italian immigrants, would become governor of the state of Connecticut. It was also noteworthy that the same May issue of the *Journal* carried on the front page a complete listing of the town's representatives to the Connecticut Legislature dating back to its incorporation in 1855. That list contained no Italian surnames, and presaged the day when Ella would become not only the first woman but also the first Italian-American to achieve that distinction.

Ella Grasso's political career began in a town which drew its name from the canal that had been built near the Connecticut River in the first decade of the nineteenth century. Shortly after the completion of the locks, which ran from Windsor Locks to Suffield, a series of major manufacturing companies grew up along the canal, creating a steady demand for skilled and unskilled labor. Many of the Irish immigrants who had come to the town in the mid-1800's worked in the newly constructed Farist and Windsor Rolling Steel Mill and the A. W. Converse Iron Foundry in Windsor Locks. Other Irish families escaping the destructive potato famine of the 1840's arrived soon afterward to augment the labor needs. By the end of the century, as social and economic conditions worsened in Southern Europe, newly immigrated Italians began to arrive in numbers to replace the Irish in the steel and textile mills. They soon became the dominant ethnic group in the town.

Ella's parents, Giacomo Tambussi and Maria Oliva, were among the hundreds of newly-arrived Italians to find employment in the bustling Windsor Locks factories. Her father worked on and off in several local mills; Maria got a job at the General Electric plant as was customary for single women who needed to help support their newly immigrated families. Like many of the other young Italians that came to Windsor Locks in those times, Ella's parents remained single for several years, working to contribute to the needs of their families as well as to accumulate a small savings with which to set up their own households. It took time for the industrious couple to gather the resources to buy a modest frame house in the Italian and Irish working-class neighborhood that bordered the factory district on the canal bank. Ownership of a house and property may have seemed particularly important to them because in their homeland, the Piedmont of Northern Italy, land was scarce and economic opportunities limited. Giacomo and Maria married late. At Ella's birth, in 1919, he was thirty-two; she was twenty-seven.

Shortly before the birth of their only child, Maria left the assembly line forever. From then on she focused her energies on raising little Ella and ran the small household on Olive Street. About the same time, Giacomo left behind his job at the Montgomery Company and the life of a factory laborer when he and his brother Natale opened a bakery which catered to Italian-American clientele. Most of the recent immigrants in the community he served still desired the fare of the "old country": bread, rice, pasta, vegetables, and fruits. Hence, Mr. Tambussi, like the other Italian shopkeepers in Windsor Locks, was able to achieve the status of a local notable by relying on immigrant tastes and traditions. His friends often gathered in the bakery or in other commercial establishments on Main Street to socialize. On religious holidays, for a small fee Ella's father, in his large ovens, cooked the hams, turkeys, and lamb that women in the neighborhood brought him.

Though the bakery was located just a few blocks away from their home, Maria did not work with her husband and brother-in-law in the store even after their daughter grew older. Giacomo probably shared common cultural attitudes of other Italian men in his generation and clung tightly to the traditional notion that women should remain in the home with the children. Now he had the means to achieve this ideal. His wife attended to the numerous domestic tasks while he operated the thriving new business establishment.

Although Maria appears to have been dominated by Giacomo, it was she who made most of the important decisions in the household. She not only managed the domestic sphere, but also exercised significant control of the family's finances. Maria has been described by many as the "driving force" in the family. A highly visible figure in the community, she was known for her temper and her strong political opinions. On the other hand, her husband, more quiet and reserved in nature, appeared to be content to provide for his family, while allowing his wife to handle the child-rearing, social, and financial affairs of the family.

Ella grew up in a closely-knit, family-centered Italian community. Both of her parents had a considerable number of relatives living in Windsor Locks. A few years after Giacomo's arrival, his younger brother, Natale, and his sister, Pierina, traveled from the small Italian town of Perleto near Voghera to join him in Windsor Locks. Ella's father remained particularly close to Natale; for not only did they run the bakery together, but they also lived in houses next door to each other on Olive Street. Giacomo, in fact, had moved his house on Main Street on rollers to the lot next to his brother's property on Olive Street. Members of Maria's family, who had come from Mello, a small town near Perleto, also lived near the Tambussi household. Ella grew up surrounded by Italian immigrants, many of whom had known her parents in Italy. Rarely a day passed when she did not see her aunts, uncles, or cousins at informal and formal family gatherings.

What the Italians called "*compari*"—a small group of friends close to the family—played an important role in the lives of Ella and her

3

parents. Like blood relatives, the family friends provided help in the business as well as companionship and support. The Luigi Colla family, one of the first to migrate from Italy to Windsor Locks, formed a close relationship with the Tambussis. Francis Draghi, a grandson of Luigi Colla who was a few years older than Ella, developed a particularly strong friendship both with Ella and her mother, Maria.

In 1924, when Ella began her elementary education at St. Mary's school, she came to know many children from Irish Catholic families, who like their Italian counterparts, earned their living in the town's factories and retail establishments along the canal bank.

During Ella's first years at St. Mary's, the Tambussi Bakery prospered as a result of an increase in the town's population. By the early Twenties, the hard work and frugality of both her parents enabled them to buy a modest summer house and property on the Connecticut shore at Soundview in Old Lyme. Later, during World War II, Giacomo had accumulated significant savings and began to provide loans to soldiers returning from service. He offered credit to secure mortgages for homes and small businesses and did so at a rate slightly lower than that offered by the town bank.

His willingness to provide credit, moreover, went beyond the desire for personal profit. In each case, he knew the parents of the young men who sought his help and drew great satisfaction from being able to assist in setting up new and productive households. Mr. Tambussi, well known in Windsor Locks and later a member of the town's credit union, became a link in the support network of the closely knit community in which he lived.

Though Ella lived in a household which was relatively better off than that of many other working-class people at the time, the Depression affected her profoundly. At age ten, when the stock market crashed, she saw its economic and social impact through the eyes of her father who was all too familiar with the widespread unemployment he had seen in Italy. Giacomo intimately knew the plight of the more unfortunate in their community. The baker witnessed daily the despair among those customers who bought the simplest bread. Despite the chidings of his brother, Giacomo consistently made larger batches of doughnuts than could be sold fresh, because he liked to sell them a

4

day later at a reduced price, a price more of his customers could afford. But Giacomo's stale doughnuts could not cure the ills of the entire community, and his daughter could not be spared some of the more visible signs of decline in the town. In the early days of the Depression, Ella saw some of her school friends being evicted from their homes on a bitter night in November. And times were not easy for the Tambussis even though her parents continued to work long hours and to practice frugality.

Just as she early learned the value of frugality, Ella learned the lesson of hard work in her years at St. Mary's School. Encouraged by her mother, who had received a little education at the Lincoln Institute, a small school for aliens in Windsor Locks, Ella worked studiously to attain top grades in math, English, geography, history, and religion. Her performance at the parochial school won her a Rockefeller scholarship to attend Chaffee, a nearby elite girls' boarding school built by a local philanthropic industrialist. A few bright students of similar working-class backgrounds in previous classes at St. Mary's had won entrance to the exclusive institution. In most cases, they needed to secure scholarships to pay for tuition. The majority of the other students at St. Mary's who could not obtain a scholarship or who did not wish to attend a university went to local public high schools.

It is difficult to conceive of a subsequent educational experience that would have been more unlike Ella's experience at St. Mary's. The student body of the Windsor Locks parochial school that lay in the heart of the town's ethnic and working-class communities contrasted sharply with that of secluded Chaffee. With its fine reputation as a preparatory school for exclusive private colleges, Chaffee and its brother institution, Loomis, drew students from wealthy families all over the Northeast. With few exceptions, Ella's classmates came from aristocratic, Protestant, and politically conservative backgrounds.

Ella knew a few students from Windsor who either attended or were attending classes at Loomis or Chaffee and this probably eased the tension of transition. Sylvio Preli, the son of a grocer who ran a shop downtown, and a close friend of the family's, had received his education at Loomis. His younger sister, Josephine, with whom Ella was well-acquainted, was two years ahead of Ella at Chaffee. Despite the slight age difference, she and Ella formed a close relationship during their years together at Chaffee.

Never completely assimilated into the non-academic sphere at Chaffee, Ella lived a seemingly dual existence during her years there. Each day she faced two worlds: the world of wealthy, aristocratic students juxtaposed with that of ethnic, working-class people. Sometimes she rode to school in a chauffeured car owned by the Coffins, a wealthy industrialist family, whose children attended Chaffee. At other times she took the train from the Windsor Locks station on the canal bank. At school she had luncheon in an ivy covered building, but she returned home every evening for supper with her family. Ella, however, seemed to have little trouble moving between these usually separate spheres.

While many of her classmates headed for Newport, Fire Island, and the like, Ella spent her summers at the family's modest beach house on the Connecticut shore. Since her family was relatively well-off, she did not have to spend the hot months of July and August in the tobacco fields as did many of her friends in Windsor Locks. At Soundview in Old Lyme, Ella and her mother visited with other Italian families who had cottages nearby. She mostly read and sometimes played first base on the mostly male softball team in Old Lyme.

The highlight of her vacations at the shore came in the summer of 1932, when she was fourteen, a few months before she was to enter Chaffee. That year, she met Thomas Grasso, a handsome lifeguard from Hartford who was four years her senior. Ella often took books to the beach to read in preparation for the instruction she would receive at Chaffee. Ella and Thomas first spoke when she was studying on the beach; she was reading Shakespeare's "As You Like It." Grasso, a "four-letter man" at Buckley High School in Hartford's South End, who "had all the girls" and who "didn't have much interest in books," became intrigued by Ella's intelligence and wit. But, given their age difference, he did not entertain notions of serious courtship.

Ella, however, persisted. She and Tom's younger brother Ernie, who had a summer milk route with his brother, often plotted together, keeping close watch over the older Grasso. Ella and Ernie, who both had learned French at school, kept each other informed of Tom's activities through notes that they left in empty milkbottles on Ella's porch. Tom, unschooled in French, could not decipher the communications and thus remained unaware of their surveillance. He even suspected a romance between his brother and Ella. After the summer ended, his friendship with Ella continued; later, he attended a few dances with her at Chaffee. Ella remained convinced of her feelings toward Grasso, and with characteristic determination to get what she wanted, declared, as the story goes, that he was "the man I shall marry." Ten summers later, she did.

Chapter Two

SOUTH HADLEY

1937-1942

Although a few women in Windsor Locks attended college, most did not. Instead they worked in jobs in the town's factories or in insurance companies in Hartford. Many of these women were from ethnic, working-class families who doubted the value of higher education and whose families probably could not afford to send their daughters to college. Even if their parents could have done so, these women were later likely to stay at home as their mothers had. Ella Tambussi's family was atypical in both respects, for her parents possessed economic and social advantages which enabled her to attend Mount Holyoke.

By the time Ella was ready to enter college in 1937, her father had become a successful businessman despite the Depression; he managed a prosperous bakery and owned property in Windsor Locks and Old Lyme. Even if Ella had not received a scholarship to attend Mount Holyoke when she graduated with honors from Chaffee, her parents would probably have had the money for her tuition at the elite woman's college. A frugal man with simple tastes, Mr. Tambussi continued to work fourteen hours a day in the bakery and saved his earnings, rarely indulging in material luxuries. He did, however, make an exception for his daughter's graduation present. Proud of Ella's accomplishments at

Chaffee, he presented his only daughter with a Persian lamb fur coat to wear at Holyoke.

Her parents provided an important impetus to Ella's educational development. Encouraged by her mother since her days at St. Mary's, Ella came to love to read and to study. Her mother, Maria, who had received a little schooling when she arrived in Windsor Locks, read avidly in Italian and English. Despite the fact that she had had no formal training in the humanities, Maria could quote Dante, Mazzini, and other Italian writers at length. Interested in politics, she read the newspapers and kept up with current affairs, sparking her daughter's later interest in political affairs.

At Chaffee, Ella had followed a college preparatory program. There she soon found she excelled in literature, language, history, and science. Placing heavy emphasis on these subjects, the school sent most of its bright students to the Seven Sisters, while Loomis prepared its young men for Ivy League universities. Going on to college was the normal course for students at these schools, so the assumption that she too would attend college seemed a natural one. Ella's plans and future might have been very different had she pursued the business program at the local public high school.

Ella found the inspiration to attend Mount Holyoke in two individuals. Josephine Preli, Sylvio's younger sister, went to Holyoke after she graduated from Chaffee. A close friend of Ella's since their two years together at Chaffee, Josephine enjoyed life in South Hadley. In addition, Ella's headmistress at Chaffee spurred her interest in the school by telling her of a new program at the college, called the "two-unit plan," which allowed students the freedom to choose their own course work rather than follow a path prescribed by the school. As a senior at Chaffee, Ella applied for admission to Mount Holyoke and sought entrance to the two-unit program.

When she entered Mount Holyoke College, Ella shaped her course of studies there according to her experience in Windsor Locks. Her mother's influence seemed evident in Ella's selection of her first year curriculum. As part of her two-unit work, she took Italian and modern European history. After taking formal grammar in the first semester, she went on to study literature, reading Dante, Mazzini, and the other poets her mother quoted. Her work in European history also found its focus in Italian history; Ella gave particular attention in that unit to Italy and the role of the papacy in its affairs.

Ella's pragmatic nature was reflected not only in her papers about the economy and the social structure of Windsor Locks that she completed early in her career at Holyoke, but also in her later choice of a major course of study in economics and sociology. In an article she wrote called "Building a Background for a Practical Life," which appeared in the alumnae magazine, Ella outlined her reasons for choosing to concentrate in the social sciences. This piece, written when she was a graduate student, cites her desire as an undergraduate to understand the social and economic problems plaguing her community and her hope to "put her new knowledge into practice."

Ella's desire to use her academic training to solve real problems may have reflected not only her familiarity with the economic and social ills of her community, but also the educational orientation of Holyoke's Economics and Sociology department. Professor Amy Hewes headed the department which strove to "keep in touch with reality and problems of the day." That the department had "vocational significance" is demonstrated in Hewes' own previous career as a social worker and as the director of Bryn Mawr Summer School for Women Workers in Industry.

Interested in labor economics, Ella took the regular course offered to other undergraduates during her junior year. She was, however, quick to supplement this academic training with field work and later with her own independent research. In extra-curricular hours she worked out educational and recreational projects with a group of working women at the local YWCA. Seeking the chance to gain knowledge about the lives of working women, she worked as an undergraduate assistant at the Hudson Shore Labor School which gave classes to women employed in domestic service or industry.

Her experience with working people brought to her attention the ineffectiveness of worker's compensation legislation in the New England states. For her senior thesis, Ella decided to concentrate her independent research on the problem of such cumbersome laws. For the project, Ella traveled to New England factories to collect data and to talk with both labor and management. Her research also brought her to several trade union meetings where she heard protest against the laws first-hand. In her one-hundred page thesis, Ella pointed to weaknesses in the existing laws: the lack of adequate coverage, the tendency to transfer costs of industrial accidents from industry to workers, the complexities of unstandardized laws, and the long delays caused by litigation. Her essay went on to suggest two major reforms in the system. Firstly, she called for the "establishment of compulsory state funds" in place of private sector insurance for compensation for work-related illness and injury. Such a reform, she claimed, would decrease delays in the enforcement of the laws caused by litigation because "private insurance companies had a business interest in defending as many claims as possible ." Secondly, she called for standardization of compensation laws. This, she felt, "could only be achieved through federal legislation."

That Ella eventually took a strenuous pro-labor stance in her thesis was not surprising: she had been aware of the conditions that made jobs scarce and workers insecure since her childhood when her father had told her the story of how he became deaf in one ear. As a young man, Giacomo Tambussi, on his way to the Montgomery factory in Windsor Locks, had been struck in the head with a piece of coal thrown by an unemployed local laborer. Her close association with working people in both Windsor Locks and South Hadley can also probably account for her strong position.

Yet it was not solely her personal experience that shaped Ella's views in her honors thesis on labor. Rather than adopt a single ideology, she borrowed selectively from separate, popular political and intellectual currents. She strongly supported the Democratic Party because of its favorable labor platform, and she applied some of the Roosevelt administration's strategies for solving social problems to her thesis. At the same time, the young Tambussi was influenced by radical literature sympathetic to labor. Although she never became a Marxist, she did become more sensitive to the plight of working people. Ella's readings of Marx combined with the tendency of the university community to be intellectually pro-labor heightened her opposition to the inadequacies in current compensation laws.

12

Ella's call for the shift of responsibility from the private to the public sector in matters of worker's compensation can be understood in the context of her support for the Depression President, Franklin Delano Roosevelt. Roosevelt, who had entered the executive office when she was thirteen, certainly came to dominate Ella's political thinking, as he did that of many other people of her generation. The President, moreover, enjoyed the height of his popularity during the years of Ella's intellectual development at Holyoke. As a leader in the campus organization behind FDR in the 1940 elections, Ella ardently admired the President's social welfare policies. Her demand for a comprehensive worker's compensation law "in line with other social security laws" mirrored the intent of FDR's legislation that emphasized federal responsibility. The concluding chapter of her thesis, in which she suggests such reforms, certainly foreshadowed the time when she, as a state executive, would call for federal administration of the welfare program.

Ella did not confine her political activism to the Roosevelt campaign. As President of the American Student Union in her last two years, she worked to promote interest in current events. This club, primarily educational in nature, conducted monthly meetings to discuss domestic and international issues of interest. As President, she organized an intercollegiate meeting to discuss the proceedings of the Dies' Committee; she established a cooperative book exchange; and she published a column in the student newspaper recommending new books on current affairs and recommending relevant lectures being held on campus. The weekly ASU article faced stiff competition by another column called "Spinach" that ran alongside of it. The latter column detailing trends in fashion on campus usually got considerably more space, dwarfing Ella's articles. Further evidence of Ella's less than successful mission to educate the students about public affairs through the club may be found in the 1940 *Llamarada*, the school yearbook. The ASU rated only a small paragraph in the extracurricular section, and the description of its activities was vague. An unidentified author wrote that the organization stressed "the national scene as well as our immediate problems." Her editors certainly knew even less about the club.

There is little doubt that Ella participated actively in the academic life of Mount Holyoke; her classmates certainly considered her an intellectual equal. Yet because she was removed from much of the college's social activity, Ella remained an outsider during her years in South Hadley. She did not play any of the sports most of her classmates participated in. Since Ella had attended Chaffee as a day student, she had not spent her afternoons and weekends at the school learning to play lacrosse, field hockey, polo, or golf. This, combined with the fact that Ella was not athletically inclined, led her to spend her afternoons at Mount Holyoke studying and pursuing her interests in politics and public affairs. Ella also did not belong to any of the social clubs on campus. The parties and dances held by these organizations formed the center of the social life at Mount Holyoke. Ella did not attend those dances. In each issue of the *Mount Holyoke News* following a class dance, all the names of couples attending were listed. In her four years as an undergraduate, the name of Ella Tambussi was absent from these lists. Inspection of the lists reveals instead a social register—women with familiar aristocratic surnames and Ivy League men from fine families. There are a few possible explanations for her avoidance of the dances. The dances required expensive formal attire, the most splendid of which was certain to be described in great detail by the author of the widely-read "Spinach" column. It is possible that Ella, who once said that her requests for material possessions "pained her mother," refused to ask for finery to wear to the balls. Or perhaps Ella's charactaristic disdain for some of the indulgences of the upper classes kept her away. Or it may have been the fact that Ella was a terrible dancer and her favorite partner, Tom Grasso, was no better. More likely, however, Ella refused to attend the college functions because she felt she could not compete with her more attractive, socially skilled classmates. She was not beautiful, and she did not possess male aquaintances at the Ivy League universities.

Though Ella could not be called unattractive, she was not pretty. Her olive skin did not have a deep golden tone; it was slightly sallow. Her long nose lacked the true Roman line. Her pin-straight hair, which she wore short and waved with a permanent, was a mousy brown. Rather short in stature, Ella's figure had neither the hard lines of an athlete nor the graceful curves of a well-endowed woman. Unlike

14

some of her classmates who shared average looks, she could not compensate by surrounding herself with male admirers. As a day student at Chaffee, Ella did not have the opportunity to cultivate many male friendships at the brother school, Loomis. Nor did her parents move in social circles in which she could meet boys who would attend private colleges as she did. And toward the end of her years there, Ella's relationship with Tom had become closer, giving her little incentive to meet other men at mixers.

Ella's apparent distaste for the dances did not keep her in her dorm room studying economics texts. Tom Grasso, the friend of her days at Chaffee and now a suitor, traveled every Wednesday from Hartford to South Hadley for their weekly date. Grasso, then working as a teacher, operated on a limited budget; he had two dollars to spend on entertainment. A dollar bought him gas for the trip. Fifty cents bought two tickets to see the Joan Crawford and Katherine Hepburn movies Ella loved. The remaining half dollar bought hamburgers and Cokes at Glessie's. Sometimes if money was particularly tight, the two would babysit for the children of her Italian professor, Dr. Giamatti, whose son, Angelo, would later become the president of Yale University.

On Friday afternoons, Ella Tambussi returned to Windsor Locks to spend the weekend with her parents. In her first two years she traveled home with Josephine Preli, whose older brother, Sy, drove them back and forth. In her last two years, Tom played chauffeur, relieving Sy of the drudgery of driving and the monotony of Ella's lectures aimed at convincing him to switch his party affiliation from Republican to Democratic. At home she would spend time with Tom, practice her Italian by translating letters from the "old country," and attend church at St. Mary's. As she had done at Chaffee, Ella again moved between two seemingly separate spheres—an ethnic, working class neighborhood and an aristocratic, upper-class college. Because she was not of the so-called "upper-class," Ella remained outside the social circles at Mount Holyoke. Yet her education at elite private schools separated her from those she knew in Windsor Locks: she could no longer be an intimate part of their community because her early experience differed so dramatically from theirs. Although the transition between these two worlds never appeared to trouble Ella, for she was well-acquainted with the language and customs of each, she remained an outsider in both.

Ella's graduation in June of 1940 did not end the frequent trips between Windsor Locks and South Hadley. Her prize-winning work in the economics department won her a fellowship for two years of graduate study at the school. During those years she continued to develop her academic interest in labor and economics. In addition to researching her master's thesis on the history of the Knights of Labor, she worked as a teaching assistant in economics. During her summer vacation she taught statistics at Columbia University in New York. As a graduate student, she remained caught up with the left labor rhetoric that had attracted her as an undergraduate. One of her students, Katherine Rorabach, recalled learning more than just standard deviations in her statistics section. Rorabach, who as an attorney would later represent members of the Black Panther Party, also learned the words to the Socialist tune "Internationale" from the young Tambussi. Still a strong supporter of FDR and an ardent admirer of his welfare capitalism, Ella clearly had ideals, but she had yet to develop a coherent idealogy.

In June of 1942, Ella left Holyoke with a bachelor's degree, a master's degree in economics, and a Phi Beta Kappa key. She departed too, deeply instilled with her alma mater's dogma of service that would stay with her longer than the words of the "Internationale." Ella did not, however, assimilate completely all of the attitudes implied in the college's ethic of selfless service to "relieve human suffering." Rather, she developed a strong distaste for the *noblesse oblige* embodied in the rhetorical question of an author in the alumnae magazine: "If we do not put public before private, who will do so?" At the same time, she maintained a strong commitment to her responsiblity to use her knowledge in the public sector. Yet the words of alumnae writers in the *Mount Holyoke Quarterly* should be taken with a grain of salt to counter the saccharin. Ten years later, Ella, who as an undergraduate pledged simply to use her academic knowledge in the public sector, changed her own rhetoric slightly when she wrote an article on public service in politics for the *Quarterly*. Her concluding statement ran:

Ours is the obligation to serve, to carry out in all conscience the purposes assigned by God to our democratic society, to join with our fellow man in charting the course of human endeavors in a sincere spirit of brotherhood and service to humanity.

Chapter Three

POLITICAL WOMAN
1943-1952

After Ella received her master's degree from Mount Holyoke, she went back to Windsor Locks. She returned to marry Thomas Grasso, as she had pledged to herself she would ten summers before. In the summer of 1942, the two took their wedding vows at St. Mary's, the parish in which Ella had been baptized and confirmed, as well as educated. Soon after their marriage, at Ella's insistence, the couple took up residence in a house directly across from her parents' home on Olive Street. This move reflected the Italian tradition of daughters setting up housekeeping close to their mothers. Shortly after their marriage, she got a civil service job in Hartford.

Ella's employment as the assistant director of research at the Connecticut War Manpower Commission after her marriage, however, was not traditional. As an executive of that agency, Ella oversaw the mobilization of labor in Connecticut's many defense-related industries. She liked her job there because she had the opportunity to apply her knowledge in labor economics and statistics. True to the Holyoke ideal, moreover, her job in this agency fulfilled her obligation to seek to benefit society through her efforts in the public sector.

Ella's husband Tom also influenced her decision to work after their marriage. Unlike many men of his generation, he did not object to, and in fact encouraged her to pursue a career outside the home. Tom, who had known Ella when she attended Chaffee and had courted her while she was at Holyoke, respected her intelligence and recognized her ambition. In turn, she inspired Tom to continue his education and even convinced him to go on to graduate school after he completed college. And Tom shared his wife's interest in public service; he worked as a teacher and as an administrator in the East Hartford public school system.

After the war ended and the agency dissolved, however, Ella left employment outside the home to begin a family. Her daughter Susanne was born in 1948 and her son Jim was born three years later. Despite the young ages of her children, Ella continued her involvement in public service by participating in community affairs. She joined the League of Catholic Women at St. Mary's and the Windsor Locks Parent-Teacher Association. An active member of the Chaffee Alumnae Association, she later took office as President. And her husband encouraged Ella to be active in community affairs. Though Tom himself did not participate in local politics and organizations, he took a strong interest in Ella's projects and gave her help and advice when she needed it.

After Tom finished teaching in June, the young family would spend the summer months at Soundview in Old Lyme. They took a small white house near the cottages where their own families had lived years before. Giacomo and Maria Tambussi left their Olive Street homestead to vacation with their daughter and two grandchildren. Ella's father kept a small garden with onions, peppers, tomatoes and squash in the front yard. He spent hours tending his vegetable patch and chatted with passersby about fertilizers and hoeing techniques. Giacomo was particularly proud of his tomatoes which ripened weeks before any in other gardens on the street. All of his neighbors, including an attractive elderly widow, were impressed with the large red fruits that grew on his tall staked plants. Giacomo's wife, however, ceased to admire the tomatoes when she learned the secret of her husband's success: as a prank, Giacomo would tie store-bought tomatoes to his homegrown plants.

Giacomo, who had a job with the White Sands beach association, was at least as meticulous a beach cleaner as he was a tomato grower. He would rise early in the morning to rake the sand smooth at the nearby beach, removing all of the debris that had washed ashore during the night. In the early evening he returned again to repeat the process. His relatives who used the beach later recalled: "You couldn't imagine that a piece of seaweed ever touched the beach."

Tom and Ella went swimming each morning with Jimmy and Susanne and spent the afternoons and weekend evenings running a small movie house. Tom ran the projector and Ella took tickets and sold popcorn. Everyone at Soundview visited their theater at least once on a rainy afternoon or evening. Her father preferred to stay at the cottage and listen to baseball games on the radio, while her mother prepared traditional Italian dishes with the summer vegetables from her husband's garden.

During these years of their marriage, Ella maintained her interest in both labor economics and politics. She served as a public representative and later as chairwoman of the state Minimum Wage Boards for business and professional workers and for industrial workers. She was appointed to the state Commission on Education and was secretary of its long-range education and fact-finding committee. Since Windsor Locks did not have a women's political organization, Ella helped found a chapter of the League of Women Voters in the town of Suffield, and worked diligently on the state League's economics committee.

The story of Ella's political affiliation is not so consistent as her dedication to public service. A former enthusiast of FDR, Ella registered as a Republican so that she could cast a vote for Sy Preli, the old family friend, who was seeking a post as chairman of the Republican Town Committee. Ella's new party affiliation did not surprise those who knew her. Despite her decidedly liberal stance on labor matters, Ella, a product of Mount Holyoke, with its emphasis on organization and efficiency, held more conservative views on fiscal issues. This combined with the fact that many other Italians in her town were Republicans did not set her apart from her counterparts on Olive Street.

Sy Preli won his bid for the position but Ella lost her interest in local politics, displaying marked indifference until the gubernatorial nominations in 1950. When Chester Bowles emerged as the Democratic candidate with a progressive labor platform, Ella left the Republican party to work for the Bowles organization formed by the Windsor Locks Democratic Town Committee. Only a year later, she "threw her bonnet into the ring," and braved the bitter primary fight over the nomination for one of the town's two General Assembly seats. Her opponent, Harry Broderick, who was a local businessman, based his campaign on an attack against Ella's apparent lack of a strong commitment to a single party.

Ella's defection from the Republican party merely demonstrated her political pragmatism or perhaps more accurately, opportunism. Upon graduation from Mount Holyoke, Ella wanted to serve on the town library board and on the Board of Education of Windsor Locks. She soon learned, however, that both boards, which were comprised of individuals such as Dexter Coffin, a leading local industrialist, Mrs. R. J. Montgomery, wife of a prominent local factory owner, and the like, did not welcome her participation. Though the aspiring public servant made her desire to serve on the library board well known, the committee ignored Ella's interest when vacancies occurred, perhaps because her qualifications exceeded those of the members themselves. Similarly, some local politicians kept Ella off the Board of Education, for they feared she would attempt to implement drastic changes in curriculum and other areas in the traditional Windsor Locks school system. They also may have resented her wish to become involved in the public school system because they knew she had been educated at parochial and private schools. She realized, moreover, that even in strong Republican years, the town consistently chose Democrats by a three-to-one margin. Therefore thwarted on the local level, she knew she could not seriously consider a successful run for office as a Republican, so she switched her affiliation.

Ella's short stint in the Democratic camp as a campaign worker for Bowles not only heightened her desire to seek political office herself but also convinced the Windsor Locks Democratic party chiefs—James R. Rabbett and John Fitzpatrick—of her talents: they became her mentors in town politics. From them she quickly learned the value of "paying her dues" through vigorous work in party activities. She also learned to appreciate the support given by her powerful political tutors. With the help of Rabbett and Fitzpatrick she was able to defeat Harry M. Broderick, who not only attacked his opponent for her change of party affiliation, but also the town committee heads for backing Ella in the Democratic primary. In that race, the voters of Windsor Locks chose J. Joseph McMahon and Ella T. Grasso as candidates for the town's two seats in the General Assembly. McMahon was the top vote-getter with 469; Mrs. Grasso got 338 to Broderick's 204.

Grasso and McMahon faced two Republicans—Philip Green and Mrs. Gladys Lynskey, a former secretary and a neighbor of Ella's on Olive Street, in the November election. The platforms written by each team were remarkably similar, reflecting the homogeneous nature of the working-class town. Both parties called for a change in state welfare laws to allow for greater benefits for those who needed them, a wage increase for state employees, a direct primary system to nominate candidates for local and state offices, and a larger allocation of funds for new school building. The Democratic program, however, had several distinctive features, due in lare part to Ella's role in its formulation. It contained a curious mix of liberal and conservative ideas reflective of those Ella had acquired during her formative years in Windsor Locks and at Mount Holyoke. The labor advocate called for "expanded social legislation for minimum wages ... worker's compensation, and unemployment insurance to promote the general welfare of all people ...." At the same time, the fiscal conservative called for a reorganization of state government to save the state money. This concern, which would become a familiar refrain in her subsequent campaigns for state office, was certainly consistent with her college training. Her economics courses at Holyoke emphasized efficiency in management as well as in production. Furthermore, Ella's upbringing in a frugal household also strengthened her commitment to competent, cost-effective administration in state departments.

The call for labor rights and reorganization by the Democratic camp did not, however, cause much controversy. Instead, another of the party's planks, one citing the need for the town's own probate court so residents would not have to travel to Hartford to settle estates, became the controversial issue of the campaign. Sy Preli, whom Ella could never convert to her side ëven in her days at Mount Holyoke, led the opposition to the plan of a separate probate court to serve Windsor Locks. He felt that the town residents were not seriously inconvenienced by the trip to Hartford and countered Ella's arguments in favor of the court, holding that such a plan would simply mean increased patronage for her party. Despite the efforts of Preli, Green and Lynskey, the Democrats triumphed, McMahon and Grasso received 1980 and 1868 votes respectively. Even with the surge for Eisenhower in Connecticut, the staunchly Democratic town supported Stevenson over Ike for President and Abraham Ribicoff over Prescott Bush, Sr., for Congress.

Shortly after the state election, Ella and her new colleague, Joe McMahon, submitted three bills to the Secretary of State's office for consideration in the 1952 session. One proposed the establishment of a probate court in the town; another called for increased state grants for the building of public schools; and the third granted free hunting and fishing licenses to veterans and those over sixty-five. After filing the bills, Ella felt prepared to go to the statehouse in Hartford.

Chapter Four

A MATTER OF MONTHS
1953-1956

Mrs. Grasso, soon to be dubbed by the *Hartford Courant* as a "house-wife politician," plunged headlong into the heated debates of the 1953 session, quickly identifying herself with labor, social, and consumer concerns. The first-term legislator and long-time labor advocate joined her Democratic colleagues in calling for expanded worker's compensa-tion, unmemployment insurance, and off-the-job sickness and accident insurance. For state employees, she strongly supported a stabilized retirement fund as well as wages and salaries comparable to those in the private sector. She also worked closely with those who spear-headed the effort to eliminate county government so that duplication of services could be avoided and worked for a more efficient welfare and health department. In addition to becoming a spokesperson for work-ing people and a critic of wasteful government, Ella developed a close association with special interest groups. She worked strenuously for increased services for the handicapped and greater aid for education. Ella further expanded her political constituency by leading the fledg-ling consumer movement at the statehouse. As a mother of two, she organized women all over the state in a drive for dated milk caps.

By the end of her first term, Ella's efforts had made friends for her among large blocks of voters in the state. Working people could not fault her flawless labor record. Business and management looked favorably on her fight for economy and efficiency in government. Professionals, liberals, and special interest groups admired her work in the areas of health, education, and welfare. Her advocacy of consumer protection, too, brought Ella bi-partisan support inside and outside the state capital. Ella's background in labor, economics, education, and social work qualified her to deal with these diverse questions. By carefully choosing her issues, she quickly gained broad-based support not only in Windsor Locks but also in other areas around the state.

Ella also began to amass political capital by using a strategy she had learned during her involvement in local politics. Her experience in Windsor Locks had taught her that political success lay not only in gaining a command of salient issues, but also in acquiring mentors within the party leadership. Unlike the rank and file female legislators who tended to achieve influence only through their work in committees, Ella also sought to attain authority by attaching herself to the powerful party elite. From the beginning of her first term, Ella successfully attempted to travel both routes to power through distinguished work in committees as well as through participation in top-level party decision-making.

Ella's early efforts could not escape the notice of Democratic State Party Chairman, John Moran Bailey. The chief architect of the Bowles victory and aptly called the "power broker," Bailey presided over party politics in Connecticut. In the Legislature he scouted talent. Boss Bailey looked for party leaders and potential political candidates; he recruited first-rate players for his soon-to-be unbeatable team. He drafted Jon O. Newman, later a U. S. Circuit Court of Appeals judge, to put together the party's legislative program at the Capitol. He spotted Abraham Ribicoff, voted by Capitol reporters as the "most promising freshman legislator" at the 1950 session and groomed him for the governorship. Boss Bailey recognized that Ella was fast becoming a powerful advocate of social causes in the General Assembly and wanted to tap her support in that area. A shrewd politician, Bailey respected her natural instincts on issues. More than a mere politician, the graduate of Harvard Law School admired her intellectual abilities. Though flexible and progressive at times, Bailey's perceptions were colored by traditional views about the role of women. He therefore did not initially perceive Ella as a potential candidate. Instead, he saw her as a behind-the-scenes, back-room, party worker and recruited her for his brain trust. Ella got her training for this new position by watching Boss Bailey play the game. As the season progressed, his signals and strategies would become second nature to her.

Bailey began the ball game in 1946 when he was chosen as State Party Chairman. Even then, the former football player at Catholic University was not new to the sport. His parents had participated in Hartford politics. Dr. Bailey served on the city's board of aldermen; his wife fought for woman's suffrage in the state. Upon graduation from law school, the young Bailey, more interested in politics than in his law practice, started his political training under Hartford's boss, "T. J." Spellacy. As T. J.'s "errand boy" in the state convention of 1932, Bailey watched the master at work in countless meetings and caucuses. Spellacy later rewarded his lieutenant with an appointment to the Democratic State Central Committee. From that position, the aspiring politician developed a strong base in Hartford as well as important contacts around the state. His work as a charter member of the Connecticut Young Democrats increased his visibility in party circles; and when John McCarthy left the chairmanship, Bailey succeeded him to the post. In Bailey's brilliant consolidation of convention forces, which would become characteristic of his political maneuvering, he captured the coveted position he would hold for three decades.

When Bailey was not traveling around the state talking to town chairmen and conducting private polls about potential candidates using slips of paper and a cigar box, one could find him at the Parma Restaurant. The Parma, located a few blocks away from the Capitol, specialized in "Italian cuisine and Connecticut politics." The Chairman held court in a small dining room that later became known as the "Bailey Room." Legislators, Hartford pols, lobbyists and anyone else who wanted to see him, could talk politics with the Boss who clenched long brown cigars in his teeth and pushed his horn-rimmed glasses on the top of his balding head. Bailey typically spent his Saturday afternoons at Scoler's Restaurant trading stories with his Hartford friends. He learned by listening to people—his party chiefs, his rank and file, and his assistant, Katherine Quinn, who reported to him the conversations she heard while riding the bus to work each morning. And he carefully examined the cigar box ballots he collected from around the state.

Chairman Bailey headed the Connecticut organization when party organizations were still powerful in the state. Until 1955, when a primary law was enacted and successfully invoked on a statewide basis in 1970, the party leadership, by commanding party conventions, determined candidates of Congressional and state offices, without public challenge.

Until the state circuit court came into existence in 1971, the judges, prosecutors, clerks and staff of town courts were chosen by town committee leaders of the political party that captured the governorship. Hence this system provided local parties with strong incentives to work for party victories. If Boss Bailey's ticket triumphed, local bosses were assured of valuable patronage.

Bailey's success at party conventions came largely from his ability to construct strong coalitions. He accomplished this by creating an ethnically and geographically balanced state ticket composed of candidates he believed could win the elections. He won over his convention delegates by convincing them that their own personal political success depended upon his team's victory. Convention delegates at the Bushnell Auditorium waited eagerly in the wings for "the Word" from Bailey and voted accordingly. To Bailey, winning—at the state convention and later at the elections—mattered most. Issues came second. The Chairman, who could be classified as a moderate, supported candidates from both ends of the ideological spectrum if he thought they could win. Bailey backed Chester Bowles, probably the most liberal governor in the state's history. And he supported Thomas Dodd for the Senate, perhaps one of the most conservative of the state's U. S. senators.

During his eight years at the helm of Connecticut's party, before Ella won her first elected office, Bailey had not only gained command of Democratic politics in the state, but he also gained considerable control in the Legislatures. When the General Assembly was in session, he spent each day at the Capitol presiding over his party's performances in the House and in the Senate. In the daily party caucuses he held before the delegates began debate on the floor, he built a consensus on that day's votes. The practice Bailey initiated, whereby a majority vote in caucus determined how all Democratic senators would vote on the floor, kept members of his party in line. It prevented the senators from making deals with Republicans to overturn the majority party in the Senate. This practice, in other words, gave Bailey considerable power over legislation. With his block in the Senate, he could hold up bills in that body until he struck deals with the Republican party leaders on legislation he wanted passed in the House where the Democrats were a minority. His troops, recognizing that strict discipline was tantamount to their success, marched up to Bailey for their "orders" as eagerly as the delegates at the state conventions waited for the "Word."

In the first months at the statehouse, Ella, like other freshman Democrats, took Bailey's orders. As the session progressed, however, she came to the fore on a variety of controversial issues, including the move for elimination of county government and the drive for dated milk caps. Recognizing a major source of power, she was careful to consult with Bailey on legislative strategies. In return, when the Chairman realized that the representative from Windsor Locks was adept at anticipating the political consequences of proposed bills, a talent he valued highly, he brought Ella into his legislative brain trust. This meteoric rise led Jack Zaiman, the *Courant's* political commentator to write:

> In a matter of months, Mrs. Grasso has gone from a seat in a crowded House of Representatives to the top level of state politics.

The Chairman and his braintrust, now comprised of C. Perrie Phillips, George Conkling, and Ella Grasso, carefully scrutinized each bill before it came up on the floor, discussing its political implications. Boss Bailey relied on Conkling for his financial expertise, Phillips for his legislative knowledge, and Grasso for her research ability and her political savvy. At the end of each of their brainstorming sessions on proposed legislation, Bailey's lieutenants would tally up the roster of bills. They noted those which would be supported, rejected, or amended by the Party; then Bailey and a few of his chosen captains would give the orders to their troops.

With characteristic care, the Chairman chose his gubernatorial candidate for the elections of 1954. After countless cigar box polls and conversations with Town Committee chairmen around the state, Bailey nominated Abraham Ribicoff, a dynamic Jewish lawyer from Hartford. Though a victim of the Eisenhower sweep in the '52 election which brought Republicans to almost every state office, Ribicoff had demonstrated by his narrow defeat that he had strong appeal to many segments of the Connecticut electorate. The former state legislator who never used terms like "the common man" or the "little people," believing they were insulting to working people, possessed strong appeal for ethnic voters in the state's industrial and urban areas. At the same time, Abe's hard work and honesty as a legislator gave him the substantial support of large numbers of native voters in the rural Yankee communities of the state. Ribicoff, with his degree from the University of Chicago Law School, had further appeal for the state's liberals and intellectuals who admired his courageous stands on civil rights.

When the time came to forge a platform for that election, Bailey entrusted the task to Grasso. After Ella's advocacy of education and health in the first session, Bailey had come to regard her as his liaison to the state's good government groups, as well as to trust her as a "sound and practical political thinker." To reward her for her work in the party in that legislative session, Bailey passed on the coveted position of platform chair to Grasso. Ella took full advantage of the post, using it to amass more political capital—valuable potential electoral support—through increased visibilty and advocacy. Grasso and the other members of the platform committee, hand-picked by Bailey, held hearings in Hartford, New Haven, Bridgeport, Stamford, and Waterbury to listen to citizens' suggestions. The heart of the platform, however, was worked out by Ella and the small committee, and major interest groups that supported the Democratic party. Past presidents and Grasso's personal interest allowed labor virtually to write its own plank. By the time the convention convened, the liberal platform passed easily because labor and most of the other major interest groups had already been consulted.

By the beginning of 1954, Boss Bailey had brought Ella into the elite circle of Democratic leadership. Grasso helped make top-level decisions about every facet of the operation of the state party. She became the editor of the State Democratic party newsletter. In addition to her duties as Bailey's chief legislative advisor, party propagandist, and platform drafter, Ella assumed the title of "assistant director of campaign activities" during Ribicoff's run for the governorship. Functionally, Bailey managed the campaign and Ella directed the press work and wrote most of the position papers. With Katherine Quinn as his technical assistant, Herman Wolf as the campaign's treasurer, and Alexander Goldfarb acting as a troubleshooter, Bailey and Grasso developed Connecticut's consummate campaign organization. Bailey's formula for success had been fulfilled: "good candidate, good issues, good organization."

Boss Bailey, convinced he had chosen an electable candidate in Ribicoff, began to work out strategies for his team. After consulting with party captains, Bailey and his forces decided to forget issues and "let the candidate's personality stand above all." Ribicoff did occasionally mention the tax increase that the current Republican administration imposed. In Fairfield county he even came out strongly against a personal income tax. The moderate Ribicoff felt he needed to distance himself from his liberal Democratic predecessor, Chester Bowles, who had lobbied for the tax. More importantly, though, he wanted to gain the support of voters in the wealthy Connecticut towns close to New York. Bailey agreed with Ribicoff's instincts on the personal income tax, but continued to focus his attention almost exclusively on building a positive public image for his candidate.

The Chairman liked the strategy of playing down issues because he enjoyed the challenge of promoting his star players on the basis of personality. A master of the stage, Bailey engineered the key event in the Ribicoff campaign. In order to win back the urban Italian vote his opponent, William Benton, seemed to be gaining, Bailey set up a fundraiser at the Wonder Bar Restaurant in Berlin for some eight hundred Italian-American Democrats. In his speech before the dinner, Ribicoff made what has come to be known in the "lore of Connecticut politics as his 'American Dream' speech," appealing directly to those that shared his working-class, ethnic background. The coming election, Abe said, would tell "whether the American dream is still alive— that any boy regardless of race, creed, or color has the right to aspire to public office ... . Where else but in the Democratic party can you find a boy named Abraham Ribicoff becoming a candidate for governor? Connecticut." By the end of the speech, the restaurant was filled with Ribicoff supporters with a renewed commitment to work for the Democratic Party. Even the party leaders who had been skeptical about Abe's religion no longer doubted his chances for victory.

One week after the American dream speech, the star of Bailey's state ticket won the governorship. In Windsor Locks the Chairman's star strategist also won reelection to the statehouse. The voters in that town, pleased by Ella's efforts in behalf of working people and consumers, nearly doubled their support for her at the polls. Ella's increasing popularity was visible not only in the total number of votes she received but also in the narrowing gap between the two representatives the town sent to the Democratic statehouse. Joe McMahon, who captured more votes than Adlai Stevenson in 1950, had gotten well over one hundred more votes than Grasso that year. In 1954, however, Ella closed the margin. McMahon managed to poll only fifteen more votes than Ella.

Though Grasso continued to be concerned with labor and consumer issues during the '54 campaign, a significant porportion of her support in Windsor Locks had come from her strong reaction to the state's handling of the hurricane that occurred a month before the election. The storm hit her town on the Connecticut River particularly hard, causing severe flood damage to public and private property. Ella, who had already developed a sohisticated mastery of the media during her work on the Ribicoff campaign, seized the occasion of a natural disaster (as she would again as governor) to gain favorable press coverage before the election. the *Hartford Courant*, one of the state's leading dailies, with correspondents at the Capitol who knew Ella as a leading legislator and a pupil of Party Chairman Bailey, carried her comments. She sharply criticized Republican Governor Lodge for his failure to establish "a competent warning system" and went on to question the efficiency of his Administration's top-level planning."

Another important media coup in her second term came when journalists reported that the coffer-conscious legislator had refused to use special license plates which allowed state representatives free rides through toll gates. Several state papers ran stories when Ella, ardent advocate of efficiency in government (who would later refuse a pay raise as governor) returned her plates to the Comptroller's office. Ella's frugality, was no doubt genuine, but the political training she received under Bailey allowed her to use the media shrewdly to enhance her public image.

Although Ella learned many political skills from Bailey, she did not always exhibit some of Boss Bailey's better qualities. Her mentor understood the value of political friendships and did not let those who crossed him on an issue become his enemies. He dismissed them with a curt "good luck to you." Unlike Bailey who forgave and forgot, Ella did not forgive. Nor did she forget. Early in the '55 session, the Legislature held another public hearing on a bill to establish a probate court in Windsor Locks. Ella had reintroduced the legislation because it had failed in her first session, and she organized the forces who favored it. Sy Preli, her old friend from her Mount Holyoke days, led those opposed. After heated debates at the hearing, Ella met Sy on the marble steps leading down from the Hall of the House. Furious at his accusations that she wanted the court solely for patronage purposes, she fumed: "Your father was a man that I admired and respected, but I would never say the same about you." A few weeks later, the bill proposing a court died in committee. Ella remained "cool" to Sy for years afterward.

Grasso's constant striving to increase her influence in the Democratic party brought her rapid success. At the end of her second session, the Laurel Club of Capitol reporters voted her "the most hardworking legislator"—the same honor Abraham Ribicoff had received as a young representative and "best state ticket material." Her party also honored her by choosing her as an assistant floor leader. Yet this was a qualified distinction. True, she was the first female floor manager selected by any party in any state, but for the first time in history, the position was shared with two assistants. The Democratic Party leadership, including John Bailey, recognized her abilities but still felt it neccessary to enlist two men to make sure the job got done.

Bailey's traditional notions about the role of women, however, did not prevent him from rewarding his advisor within the institutional framework of the Party for her loyalty and hard work. In the summer of 1955, when the convention to appoint a committee man and woman for the Democratic National Convention approached, Bailey chose to support Grasso over the female incumbent, Dorothy Satti of New London. Weeks before the convention, the Chairman made it clear that he was behind Grasso. When the Party caucused, Boss Bailey's choice triumphed over Satti by 35 to 2.

Although the post of national committee woman usually meant anonymity on the state political scene, Grasso maintained a high level of visibility in Connecticut, despite the fact that she had declined to seek a third term in the Legislature. In Connecticut she continued to amass her political capital. Her party work—publishing the newsletter, researching legislative questions, planning campaigns, and advising the Chairman—kept her at the Capitol daily. Now a familiar face in the Bailey entourage, Ella received regular mention in the columns of widely-read Capitol political commentators like Jack Zaiman at the *Hartford Courant*, Jim Mutrie at the *New Haven Register*, and Alan Shoenhaus at the *Bridgeport Telegram*.

Common themes echoed through the pieces written by these members of the Capitol press corps. They focussed on her hard work, intelligence, her rapid success within the party and her sex. The Hartford papers proved particularly laudatory. In a full-page story on Ella, it portrayed the happy "housewife" at home with her children preparing dinner at the electric stove. The accompanying article detailed her meteoric rise within the party ranks. Jack Zaiman, the *Courant's* political columnist, who had predicted that Ella would be the first Phi Beta Kappa to serve at the Democratic Convention, marveled:

> How she (Grasso) runs a household is a mystery to many.
> She is at the General Assembly every day, takes part in party

caucuses, gets material for weekly bulletins she sends out to party members, keeps her eyes and ears open and otherwise puts in a great deal of time.

Grasso learned early to consciously cultivate the image of the house-wife politician and to maximize her support among her female constituents through her work on legislation relating to eduction, health, and consumer affairs. Ella's long membership in the League of Women Voters taught her the value of bi-partisan support. Her frequent appeals to what some considered the immediate concerns of women, such as health and consumer issues, not only allowed her to cut across party lines, but also provided her with the added benefit of enlisting the support of those who would otherwise view her as simply an ambitious politician. Yet unlike other female legislators who tended to focus almost exclusively on "women's" issues, Ella's legislative activity encompassed other areas outside of education and health. On the one hand, she could gain the confidence of women in the home by her efforts in family-related areas, while on the other, she could garner votes from their husbands who could admire her advocacy of labor rights and efficiency in government.

Chapter Five

MADAME SECETARY
1957-1970

Tired of her traveling duties as national committee-woman, Ella began to seriously consider running for elected office in 1958. The next rung up on the ladder of traditionally female political positions was the office of the Secretary of State. For almost twenty years, women in the state had held the post with little interruption. Mentioned prominently as a candidate for that position as early as 1954, the cautious Windsor Locks politician finally acquired the confidence to test her widespread popularity on the state level.

A number of other women "threw their bonnets into the ring"—as the *Courant*'s reporters were fond of saying—for the nomination in both parties. High interest in the office was a testament to its attractiveness. As a state's chief elections officer, the Secretary of State had the happy task of traveling around Connecticut urging people to vote. The Secretaryship offered the golden opportunity for high visibility without the liability of controversy. Since the Secretary was responsible only for the administration of the election laws, it was difficult to make enemies. Further, the position had come to be regarded among women as a stepping stone for higher office. Chase Going Woodhouse, for example who held the office from 1941 to 1943, went on to win a Congressional seat.

Two women in the elite ranks of the Democratic party emerged as major contenders. Gertrude O'Donnell, the Vice Chairwoman of the Democratic State Central Committee and Bea Rosenthal, the state central committeewoman from the 20th district, joined Ella in the preconvention race. Early on in that campaign, however, as had been the case in the previous election for national committeewoman, Bailey made clear his choice. Bailey wanted Ella at the Capitol to command the troops since his campaign to nominate the young senator from Massachusetts, John F. Kennedy, for President, had begun to take him away from Connecticut more frequently. Boss Bailey also needed Ella to provide the ethnic balance for his ticket headed by Abraham Ribicoff, a Jew, and Thomas Dodd, an Irish Catholic. In May, writers close to Bailey reported Grasso to be "holding the lead for the nomination." When the party caucused in August with the Chairman behind her, Ella won a decisive victory.

Though she had a clearly articulated program, which included pledges to hold more frequent conferences for local election officials, to simplify voter registration procedures, and to launch expanded voter education programs, Ella followed the Bailey formula and played down those issues. Instead she plugged the Domocratic party and the platform she had helped draft. Her campaign speeches lauded Governor Ribicoff and his progressive record. The party's platform and record, both subjects she knew intimately, at least provided her with a storehouse of material to enliven the traditionally staid, non-controversial race for chief elections officer.

The state elections that year did not lack excitement for the Democrats. Governor Ribicoff, who had won his first term by only a few thousand votes, defeated his Republican opponent by almost 250,000 votes, sweeping the entire state ticket with him. An unheard- of seven out of eight Congressional seats went to Democrats. And to the Chairman's delight, not only did the Democrats capture control of the state senate, but for the first time in over fifty years, the House of Representatives went Democratic 141 to 138—a feat thought virtually impossible given the legislative malapportionment.

Bailey's new task now lay before him—to turn his Democratic troops in the House into a dedicated, loyal army. In order to create a strong sense of unity in his frequent caucuses, Bailey used a number of effective tactics. He reminded the legislators of the debt they owed to Ribicoff's landslide victory. The Boss also reminded his ranks that the Republicans expected them to falter in their first session in power. His efforts proved successful. As one freshman legislator, Robert Satter, in that session wrote:

> John Bailey was like Knute Rockne in the Democratic House caucuses. He so exhorted the Democrats to party unity that we used to pound on the desks and roar out of the caucus room for Republican blood.

The Chairman also appealed to the Democratic legislators in a more basic way. When the hours grew longer as the session progressed, he provided sandwiches and coffee for his troops. They gathered in the command post he set up in Secretary of State Grasso's office where Boss Bailey presided as patriarch over his developing Democratic family.

If Bailey was the father figure in the party, Ella was the party's mother. Freshmen legislators, many of whom expected Ella to be "the Dragon Lady" because of her high position in the Democratic leadership, quickly became acquainted with the warm and personable Mrs. Grasso. She took them under her wing, running workshops at the Parma to acquaint them with the party's platform and program. The new lawmakers soon learned Ella was more than a "nice housewife" and came to seek her counsel and advice. Her office door was always open and her coffee pot filled. Members of the rank and file could get a cup of her famous "forty-three bean" brew, get her opinion on a particular issue, or try out an idea for a bill before they brought it to Bailey.

The Secretary of State's suite, a few feet down the hall from the Governor's office, became the unofficial headquarters for the party's high command at the Capitol. There Bailey, Grasso, and the other members of his legislative braintrust, Jon Newman, Perrie Phillips, and George Conkling, would meet to discuss pending legislation. Every morning when the General Assembly was in session, party leaders in the House and the Senate would report to Ella's office to receive their "marching orders." Typically, the party whips would be greeted by Bailey, who sat with his legs up on the desk and glasses pushed up on his head. Flanked on either side by Ella and Perrie Phillips, both of whom wore *their* glasses pushed up on their foreheads, he gave directions, waving his ever-present cigar as he spoke. Later in the day, the three might hold a "kitchen cabinet" meeting with Ribicoff and his top aides to map out long-term legislative strategies.

Proof of Boss Bailey's "legislative legerdemain" lay in the Democratic record at the end of the 1959 session. He had kept his thin majority together to pass two of the most controversial bills in the session—court reform and abolition of county government. Though Bailey certainly did not relish the idea of losing valuable patronage, mounting pressure from liberal forces and a dare from the Republican State Chairman, Ed May, caused him to marshal his forces to make counties obsolete. He held every one of his votes in line while five in May's camp defected, giving him the winning margin.

It was not only Bailey's shrewd political maneuvers that brought Ribicoff a spectacular record. Ella's reminders of the party's platform commitments, which the Chairman noted "she shrill-voiced .... continually," led him to produce similar victories in the areas of consumer protection, mental health and civil rights. In her new role as the "conscience of the Democratic Party," she pushed successfully for the mentally retarded, and she gathered enough support in the General Assembly to pass the first law in the country establishing mandatory public education for retarded children. The law also established a department of mental health and introduced a plan to relieve the financial burdens of parents with children residing in training schools. With her vigorous support and Ribicoff's leadership, Connecticut passed one of the first laws banning housing discrimination on the basis of race, religion, or nationality, a law which helped the governor win nation-wide acclaim.

Significantly, Ribicoff also kept his promise not to raise existing taxes or to impose a personal income tax. The major legislation enacted by his party in the General Assembly did not cost money. Abolition of county government, the reorganization of the executive branch, and the establishment of professional state courts would actually save the state money. Faced with increasing costs and bound by his campaign pledge not to levy further taxes, the governor resorted to diverting thirty million dollars from the highway fund and collapsing many special funds to balance the budget. In what would be his last term in office, Ribicoff kept his promise by manipulating existing financial resources. He established the practice of converting categorical funds into cash for the General Fund.

Shortly after the General Assembly adjourned, relieving her of her legislative duties for a time, Secretary of State Grasso launched her own program. At a conference of some five hundred town clerks and registrars, Ella announced that she and her elections division attorney, Amalia Toro, would make personal visits to discuss questions about administration of the state's election laws. This represented a reversal in previous policy which dictated that local officials travel to Hartford with their problems. Her announcement came as somewhat of a shock to Toro since the Secretary had not even discussed the plan with her prior to her speech at the conference. Ella, as she explained later, had wanted to propose something exciting but had little inspiration until the evening before when she conceived the idea. Rather than simply explain a proposal for new voter registration procedure and tell of her plan to write a handbook for voters, Ella wanted to capture the attention of the media. Her efforts were rewarded with articles in every major newspaper and television coverage on all the Connecticut channels.

In addition to the attention she got immediately after her address, the Secretary knew she would continue to get press coverage every time she and Attorney Toro traveled to a particular town when local newspapers would report on their visit. These visits would give her the opportunity to meet city officials and citizens in every town and city in the state. In each municipality she planned to meet with the clerk and registrar, as well as with the mayor or first selectman and with interested citizens. Traveling in this largely public relations capacity, she could also make new contacts and renew old ones within her party at the local level all over the state. Her innovative new policy represented a deliberate effort not only to expand the office of the Secretary of State but also to enhance her own influence and broaden her power base.

While scoring political and legislative success in the General Assembly, both Bailey and Ribicoff had begun to "cast their eyes beyond Connecticut's borders toward the national scene." At the 1956 presidential convention, they emerged as two of the most vocal supporters of Senator John F. Kennedy. Their persistence over the following four years paid off handsomely in 1960—the young President named Bailey as Chairman of the National Democratic party and Ribicoff as Secretary of Health, Education, and Welfare.

Ribicoff's subsequent resignation from the governorship marked a period of change within the state party. During his short tenure as governor, he had single-handedly changed its "face and soul." When he began his first term in 1954, the party had been composed of Poles, Italians, and blacks in poor to lower middle income groups. Since the ascendancy of FDR, the Connecticut Democratic Party had drawn the bulk of its support from labor and liberal groups whose heroes were men like the progressive Governor Chester Bowles. Ribicoff moved the party away from the liberal tradition because his style of campaigning and governing were directed toward a broad moderate center. In attempting to appeal to the middle, as former University of Connecticut President Homer Babbidge noted, the party under Ribicoff and Bailey ceased trying to sell its progressive ideals to independents and moderates, and was guided instead by the moderating political facts of life.

John Bailey decided to stay on as Chairman in Connecticut. The Boss knew, however, that he needed to elevate his most trusted lieutenants to take over the command when he was attending to national party politics. He made Ella the overall legislative field commander. As always, she continued to concentrate on platform issues, but now acted for Bailey as the senior strategist in the General Assembly. Her own political horizons began to expand beyond the state when she served as a member of the platform drafting committee at the 1960 Democratic National Convention. In addition to her work at the statehouse and in the party, Ella began to write the speeches Bailey gave in his capacity as national chairman. As a reward for her efforts, the Chairman asked President Kennedy to appoint her to the Board of Foreign Scholarships. This event marked her first appearance on the national scene.

Ella found the going rough in the '61 session of the General Assembly without Bailey in Connecticut. Her speechwriting cut into the time she had to devote to the Legislature. The Democrats faced a large majority of Republicans in the House. Former Lieutenant Governor John Dempsey, who had taken over when Ribicoff left for Washington, found his predecessor's "balanced budget" to be unbalanced by fourteen million dollars. Dempsey requested a reduced budget and tax increases, but the Republicans passed a higher spending package and refused to raise taxes. Neither Ella nor Bailey's two other captains, former Senate Majority Leader Arthur Healy and C. Perrie Phillips, nor Governor Dempsey could make the Legislature obey, leaving the Republicans to pass the major part of their platform. Eight days before the close of the session, the Boss flew back from Washington to bail out the Democrats. He broke the legislative logjam at an unprecedented caucus of Republican and Democratic leaders by negotiating a compromise with the Republican leadership, allowing for increases in the salaries of state employees and welfare budgets as well as grants for urban renewal.

Bailey, by his efforts in the last eight days of the session, saved the day for the Democrats. In the '62 election the party lost only eight seats in the House, and Dempsey narrowly defeated Alsop, the Republican candidate for governor. Ella, however, did not appear to need the Chairman's help. She led the state ticket, winning reelection by over eighty thousand votes. Her huge plurality was nearly three times that of the popular former governor now elected to the U. S. Senate, Abraham Ribicoff.

Ella's stunning reelection success in '62 had much to do with her shrewd use of her office as Secretary of State. By the time her second campaign began, she had completed her visits to each of the state's towns and cities, gaining visibility and increasing popularity with every stop. Her relatively light official duties at the Capitol, moreover, allowed her to spend long hours working for the party as well as for special interest groups, again maximizing voter recognition and support. During her first term, she became known for her advocacy in the General Assembly of the rights of the mentally retarded and of blacks. Further, because of the fact that Ella's official duties as Secretary of State were essentially administrative and transcended partisan considerations, the position enabled her to take credit for the successful crusades she launched in the Legislature without taking the blame for measures that failed.

Grasso, like Bailey's other pupil, Abe Ribicoff, successfully created an image with which to garner grass roots support. While Ribicoff tended to cultivate the classic notion of the "poor boy made good," Ella appealed to both native Yankee and ethnic voters alike by emphasizing the frugality she had learned in her childhood. She refused to spend state money on the customary new car to be used by the Secretary of State, Ella insisted that her predecessor's car was still serviceable. Citizens around the state applauded this gesture, remembering when Ella returned her special legislator's license plates which let her ride free through tolls. Later, in her first term, the Secretary caused an uproar when she refused to attend the annual meeting of the National Association of Secretaries of State, claiming that it would be not only a "waste of time," but also a "waste of taxpayers' money."

Though her frequent displays of frugality were part of a conscious effort to gain grass roots appeal, her decidedly frumpy dress was not. That she gave little thought to her appearance was evident in her careless attire. Her clothes were baggy and often sported loose buttons. Her hems were uneven and her stocking usually had runs in them. Her short cropped hair was almost always mussed and her flat shoes lacked style. Her lack of concern for fashion, however, did not repel but rather endeared her attentive public to her. This sentiment was reflected in an article by the fashion editor of the *Courant* who noted that Mrs. Grasso had only two campaign dresses, but excused her because her busy political schedule did not allow her adequate time to assemble a complete wardrobe.

Ella maintained a high visibility as Secretary of State. She travelled around Connecticut lecturing about proposed changes in election laws. She spoke at countless meetings of civic groups and political organizations. A favorite activity was giving tours to the many school children who visited the Capital. When she spotted a group of visitors outside of her first floor office, she would invite them in to see the paintings of Connecticut scenes in her office.

Although Ella never inherited her father's ease with growing things, she loved wildflowers. She kept a trowel and boxes in the back of the state car she used to travel to her official engagements. When she spotted wildflowers along the highway, she commanded the trooper driving the car to stop, while she clambered up the hill alongside the highway with her trowel in hand. Ella would dig up the flowers and keep them in boxes until she could transplant them to her gardens in Windsor Locks and Old Lyme.

With Bailey still in Washington as Party Chairman, the '63 session was organized much like the one in 1961. Ella again took over as the chief legislative commander. Governor Dempsey, who had gained increased support culminating in his election in '62, could now exert more influence in the Assembly. But with Bailey's continued absence and with a larger Republican majority in the House, Grasso and Dempsey had little optimism with respect to their program. Their hopes plummeted further when the Republicans, in an effort to diminish the autocratic rule of John Bailey, launched two investigations into the state's land purchasing and insurance policies. While the land purchasing probes revealed nothing, the insurance investigation uncovered Democratic misdeeds which were damaging to Bailey. Though the Chairman maintained his position and power in the state, he was unable to aid Grasso and Dempsey in the General Assembly to the degree that he had in 1961. Consequently, the Republicans refused to raise taxes as Dempsey desired and cut the governor's budget, denying funds to education and welfare. The Democrats did manage one major victory, due largely to the joint efforts of Dempsey and Grasso—their law barring discrimination on the basis of race and religion was expanded to cover all housing units.

The relationship between Dempsey and Grasso, however, was not as cordial as their close association in the Legislature implied. Ella considered Dempsey to be her intellectual inferior and did little to conceal that fact. The Governor, well aware of her sentiment, came to deeply resent her for it. Despite their mutual distaste, the two followed the example of Bailey and Ribicoff, both of whom had numerous personal differences. They maintained a working relationship out of political necessity. Dempsey needed the Secretary's support in order to rally the Legislature behind his progressive program. Grasso needed the Governor's support to continue her activities in the Assembly as well as in the

Party. Hence, Dempsey had to tolerate her superior attitudes and sometimes unconstructive behavior at his "kitchen" cabinet meetings, while Ella had to tolerate Dempsey's occasional political ineptness.

Ella's working relationship with other people outside the party and the Legislature also proved stormy. She and her elections attorney, Amalia Toro, had frequent heated disagreements over small and large policy questions. Staff workers in the Secretary of State's suite and in other offices around the Capitol were alerted to an argument between the two strong-willed women when doors began to slam and loud talk gave way to screaming and yelling. Since a truce was not always crucial, either to the functioning of the office or to her political ambitions, Madame Secretary stubbornly went for days barely speaking to her chief assistant. The relationship, however, did have its happier moments when the two women exchanged huge homemade birthday cards or sabotaged each others offices with large cartoons.

As a leader of the Resolutions Committee at the Democratic National Convention in 1964, Grasso managed to maintain a good working relationship with her Co-Chairman, Carl Albert, then the Majority Floor Leader in the House of Representatives. Though she "didn't do much presiding," as the *Hartford Courant* noted, Albert publicly acknowledged her services: "The chair will take this opportunity to express his personal appreciation to his co-chairman who has done so much of the work—the honorable and gracious Mrs. Grasso." It was also said that Albert privately told Secretary Grasso that if she ever came to Washington as a member of the House of Representatives he would see to it that she got assigned to a powerful committee where she could put her talents to good use.

By 1964, the possibility of Ella's running for Congress was far from remote. Before the state convention of that year, a coalition of Democratic leaders from Litchfield county seriously considered drafting Grasso as a candidate for the sixth district seat. The coalition, organized to protect the interests of small towns, like Ella's native town of Windsor Locks, against the cities of New Britain, Bristol, and Torrington, was unsuccessful in its attempt. Ella quickly endorsed Bailey's choice, Bernard Grabowski, who was subsequently nominated. Because the Chairman needed a Polish-American to balance his ticket, and to challenge Grabowski would undoubtedly cause Democratic disunity, Ella followed Bailey's rules. Yet, Bailey, despite his traditional views, could not ignore Ella's rising support which she demonstrated in 1962 when she led the state ticket in her stunning reelection race.

Bailey's efforts as National Chairman proved supremely successful in 1964. His candidate, Lyndon Johnson, triumphed over Barry Goldwater. He won by almost twenty percent in Connecticut, pulling in all of the state's six Democratic candidates for Congress. LBJ's landslide, however, could do little for the Democrats in the Legislature. The Republican majority remained because the State Supreme Court had ordered that the Legislature be held over while the malapportionment that gave small towns a heavy advantage was being corrected. To comply with the edict of the Court, calling for a Constitutional convention, Governor Dempsey appointed Ella to a commission to prepare it. This gave her the opportunity to greatly enhance her political position, and at the same time to rise above mere politics in the noble effort to rewrite the Constitution.

Her strong commitment to remedy the "absolutely shameful" situation that existed in the Constitution state, as well as her desire to be at the forefront of a major state issue, won her the chair of the planning commission. After the delegates had been selected, they chose Grasso—the grand dame of conferences, caucuses and committees—to be the floor leader for her party at the convention.

When the convention convened on July 1, 1965, the two party chairmen, under the leadership of Bailey and May and the two floor leaders, Grasso and Alsop, and the delegates put together a reapportionment plan and created a process for reapportionment every ten years. The provision, which dictated that each town have one representative if its population was under 5,000 and two if over that number, was struck and replaced by a far more equitable method of representation based solely on population. This meant that each new assembly district would get only one representative. Many small towns were combined to form such districts.

Most towns found this bitter medicine hard to swallow. As a resident of a small town, Ella understood this sentiment. Indeed, the situation

47

made her personal position quite difficult, for she depended on the strong political support of Windsor Locks and the small towns surrounding it. Furthermore, when Windsor Locks had risen to a population of over 5,000, she had been the first Representative elected to the resulting second seat. In other words, her political career might have never gotten off the ground in 1952 if the Constitution had been changed fifteen years earlier. Ella did believe that the "greater good" would be better served by the institution of the "one person one vote" system; but always the shrewd politician, she hedged when necessary to keep her small-town support. To make this reapportionment medicine more palatable, she and her Republican counterpart, Meade Alcorn, deliberately kept the language of the new provision vague. Their key passage read:

> The establishment of districts in the General Assembly shall be consistent with federal constitutional standards.

When the convention settled the reapportionment question, the delegation moved to update the antiquated eighteenth century document.

As she had done with the state and national platforms, Ella made the Constitutional convention a forum for the advancement of human rights and for the advancement of her own political career. She played a major role in drafting amendments, including anti-segregation provisions and a guarantee for free public education, which won her acclaim from liberal, education and civil rights groups. In addition to working for these high goals, she also cooperated enthusiastically with Bailey to secure the strong hold of Democratic power in the state's constitution. Their power brought the passage of a little-publicized provision to permit voting by party lever—"the pillar of party power"—to be included in the document, making it impossible for the Legislature to remove the practice except by constitutional amendment. When voters turned out to accept the amendment that December, it was doubtful they understood all they were getting.

No sooner had Ella given her notes on the convention to the archives at Central Connecticut State College than she took up the task of writing the '66 platform. The *Hartford Courant* noted that again Ella Grasso was "the girl called to front and center." Characteristically, the paper wondered how, with her responsibilities as a platform architect and "think man" in Bailey's entourage, "Madame Secretary still had time for family life." Bailey left Ella to her own devices on the drafting of the platform while he worked on putting together a winning state ticket.

In the early fall of 1966, Ella devoted many hours to the task of drafting the party's platform. She did not neglect work on her own candidacy for Secretary of State, although her re-election was eminent and continued to hone her campaign skills. Because her duties did not require the Secretary's constant presence in her Capitol office, Ella spent most of her days traveling to towns across the state, speaking about changes in election laws, but more often about her reelection. A trip to Middletown in early October demonstrated her developing personal political style and her increasing rapport with her state-wide constituency.

Ella left her Hartford office at 8:30 a.m. and drove to Middletown in her rented campaign car covered with bumper stickers and posters. Middletown was a city she felt particularly comfortable in—the town's heavily ethnic, Catholic and working-class character made it seem very similar to her hometown of Windsor Locks. After coffee at the Democratic headquarters in the Northend where most of the businesses were owned by Italians and Italian-Americans were located, Ella gave a brief interview to a local radio reporter who wanted to know about her office's re-examination of the state's absentee voting laws. When she finished the ten-minute taping, the Secretary anxiously began to begin the day's campaigning at the town's three garment factories.

Ella had chosen to visit the clothing factories because they were among the City's largest employers, but also because most of the employees were among her most loyal supporters. Nearly all of the Italian-American women who worked in the garment companies knew the stories of Ella's beginnings in Windsor Locks. No doubt they respected her college education and career in state politics that gave her a comfortable middle-class living standard, but they also greatly admired her achievements as a woman politician. Ella spoke Italian and possessed an unintimidating physical appearance. When she walked up to the third floor of the Middletown Rubber Company Building occu-

pied by the Carmella Coats garment shop, the women rose from their
sewing machines and applauded their sister. Ella bowed her head
modestly as she smilingly acknowledged their greeting. The Secretary
walked easily through the cutting tables and sewing machines. She
watched several skilled workers demonstrate cutting and stitching
techniques and told onlookers about her mother who had once worked
in a mill.

Moved by the enthusiasm of the garment workers, Ella spent several
hours wandering down Middletown's Main Street which encompassed
the Northend with its many business establishments that were run by
the City's ethnic residents. For her first stop, the Secretary selected the
Terminal Barber Shop, because, as she told her campaign aides, "My
father-in-law was a barber." She shook hands with a mechanic over the
transmission of a car at the Citgo Gas Station and with the butcher at
Joe Russo's market. Then another barber shop, more markets, more
handshakes, and a photograph with a brownie troop at St. Mary's
School. By two o'clock she had visited every storefront on Main
Street. She substituted a pair of heels for her buckskin flats and
drove off to Woodbridge for a fundraising tea party with her Mount
Holyoke alumnae.

When the General Assembly convened under the new constitution
after the '66 election, Democrats dominated the House by a large
margin. Governor Dempsey was reelected to his second full term by an
impressive plurality of over one humdred thousand votes. Ella led the
winning ticket by almost one hundred and fifty thousand votes to
capture her third term as Secretary of the State. Further, the party
managed to capture all but one Congressional seat. Significantly, Bernard Grabowski, the incumbent Congressman in the sixth district in
which Ella resided, lost to his Republican opponent, Thomas Meskill.
Democratic leaders, Bailey among them, began to look to Grasso to
regain the seat in the next election.

One of the skills Ella had learned from her mentor, which had
accounted for part of her past political success, made her a top contender for the sixth Congressional seat. She early learned the merit of
Bailey's favorite adage: "The mark of a successful politician is one that
finds out where the parade is going, takes one step out in front of the

band and declares himself the leader." When she sensed the public's attitudes shifting in favor of expanded rights for the mentally retarded and later for blacks, Ella stepped out quickly so as to appear to be leading the parade. Mrs. Grasso again took the opportunity to lead the band on campaign finance disclosure laws in 1967 when aides to Thomas Dodd charged that the senator had spent almost $200,000 raised at fundraising events for his personal use rather than his campaign expenses. In the same year, Ella introduced legislation making such behavior illegal and established stricter reporting procedures.

Similarly, she shrewdly recognized her state's strong sentiment against the war in Vietnam and attempted to champion opposition to it at the 1968 Democratic National Convention. As co-chair of the platform committee, Ella worked tirelessly for a "peace plank." Unhappy with the wording of the emerging party plank, Ella offered a much stronger alternative to the dismay of Boss Bailey who felt she and Abe Ribicoff were seriously undermining Democratic unity with their vigorous anti-war efforts at the convention. Her amendment called for an immediate end to the bombing and for American insistence that the government of South Vietnam begin negotiations with the National Liberation Front. The Party, unwilling to take such a strong stand, refused to pass her proposal. Though the measure failed, her efforts did not go unrewarded, for she won the support of thousands in her home state who opposed the war.

Ella's push for a peace plank at the party convention represented one of the few times she ever crossed Bailey on an issue. Though Grasso, like Ribicoff, appeared prepared to risk incurring the Chairman's wrath and losing her political capital because she saw the opportunity for personal gain, her decision to act in defiance of the Boss remained a difficult one. Ella held a perspective on the issue wholly different from Ribicoff's and Bailey's. As a woman and a mother of a draft-age son, she could better understand the human costs of war as perhaps her male counterparts could not. She did not feel, as many of her colleagues who had served in World War II or Korea, that young men should die in a foreign war that served no vital interest of the United States. In the context of a convention dominated by men who insisted that young men should go to war as they had, Ella's stand, which directly opposed

Bailey and the policy of the Democratic Party, was a courageous one.

As the election approached, the pols at the Parma spent long lunch hours speculating about whether or not Mrs. Grasso would run for Congress in 1968. For many, her candidacy appeared to be a foregone conclusion since November of 1966. At the end of 1967, however, rumors circulated that she would not run. The Chairman clearly wanted Ella to go to Congress and was prepared to give his whole-hearted support if she decided to enter the race. He considered her to be the best candidate and the one with the best chance of winning. Finally, when she was forced to state her intention in February, Grasso said she would not run. A few months later, she let it be known to Bailey that she was interested in a position on the Public Utilities Commission, while candidates began to surface to take her place as Secretary of State.

Mrs. Grasso declined to run for Congress because she said she could not leave her family—"her obligations as a wife, a mother, and a daughter would not permit her to go to Washington." It was not difficult for those who knew about her personal situation to understand this sentiment. Her husband Tom had suffered two severe heart attacks in late 1967. Though he returned to his position as school principal, his doctors advised against the type of strenuous activity which would certainly be involved in a Congressional campaign. The Grasso's college-age daughter had almost lost her life in a car accident two years before. Though Suzanne too was back at school, her anxious mother worried constantly about her condition as well as about her younger son Jim. Ella's parents, both in their eighties also had begun to demand considerable time and attention. Raised in the Italian tradition which taught that the family was always most important, Ella appeared to believe that she could not fulfill this responsibility if she spent most of each week away from Connecticut.

The Parma pols, who refused to take what their fellow politicians held out at face value, offered a different set of reasons for Grasso's decision. Some said she feared a Republican sweep; others said she feared losing her first election; still others felt she could not go along with the current President's Vietnam policy as Bailey would expect her to do. Whatever the reason, her choice was a shrewd one. The incumbant Republican candidate, Thomas Meskill, won the sixth Congressional seat by a huge plurality of almost fifty thousand votes. Ella continued in her position as Secretary of State.

Many of these political observers at the Parma also felt that her career would wane if she remained in Hartford as the Secretary of State. Twelve years in the largely symbolic office, she had served the longest term since Thomas Day who held the post from 1810-1835. Bailey's politics had played a large role in her long tenure there. His traditional notions about womens's roles coupled with his sense of what the Connecticut electorate was ready for, kept him from backing Ella to run for an office higher than a Congressional seat, which was the highest office women had achieved in the state.

In early 1970, when Mrs. Grasso's name began to be mentioned prominently as the candidate to replace Thomas Dodd for the Senate, Bailey's politics again contributed to Ella's decision not to seek that nomination. Two factors guided the Chairman's opposition to Ella's possibly candidacy for that office. Firstly, a woman had never held the office of Senator or governor in the state and such a risk seemed too large in the uncertain times of the new decade. Secondly, he was already taking a risk in the '70 election by supporting Emilio D'Addario for governor, because with the exception of Abraham Ribicoff, the state party had in recent years always had Irish Catholics as candidates for governor and senator. D'Addario also did not want two Italians on the ticket. Grasso, knowing she would not fare well at the convention without the Chairman's and gubernatorial candidate's support, chose the more secure path and decided instead to run for Congress in the sixth district to regain the seat held by Republican Thomas Meskill, who was leaving that office to run for Governor. With Bailey's backing, Ella handily defeated Arthur Powers of Berlin and Andrew Denuzze of New Britain at the convention. Her two opponents each received only twenty-odd votes to her 136.

Mrs. Grasso's Congressional campaign called forth an important skill she had learned as a student at Chaffe and Mount Holyoke—to move with ease from an ethnic, working-class community to an intellectual, upper-class community. Her hybrid district that straddles Hartford and Litchfield counties was made up of industrial cities and wealthy hamlets where the"clover of the clever and the celebrated" lived. Among its constituents were Arthur Miller, William Buckley, and William Styron. Ella chose her issues accordingly, pledging to fight the economic problems plaguing the manufacturing towns of Torrington, Bristol, and New Britain. To attract those who lived the "bucolic life" in Litchfield, she promised to pursue an end to environmental pollution. Her campaign trail took her to factory gates and Italian festivals, to garden clubs, and to fancy fundraising parties given by Paul Newman. She did not appear as an outsider in either realm.

This winning ability combined with the backing of Boss Bailey's organization made her a strong candidate. The Chairman had enlisted Abraham Ribicoff to endorse Mrs. Grasso on radio advertisements and Maine's Edmund Muskie to accompany her on a campaign tour. But Boss Bailey lost little sleep over the sixth district seat, for by that time, "Ella" had already become a household name, synonymous with caring government. Her years of work in the General Assembly and on the Democratic state and national platform committees brought Mrs. Grasso the necessary support of ethnics and Yankees, blue collar workers and intellectuals, urban and small town dwellers, lower and upper income groups, the elderly and the young.

Bailey's fears about D'Addario proved correct. His opponent, Thomas Meskill, an Irishman, defeated him decisively. The Republicans also captured two congressional seats and six more seats in the statehouse. Boss Bailey did, however, get some good news that election day when he learned the Democrats had retaken the sixth congressional seat. Despite Meskill's strong performance, Ella managed to win by a small margin of a few thousand votes over her opponent Richard Kilborn. Her victory was, nonetheless, impressive, for the Democrats lost the governor's race in that district by over thirty-four thousand votes.

Chapter Six

MRS. GRASSO GOES TO WASHINGTON
1971-1974

"So this is the Gridiron dinner.
Big deal. To think I gave up a
Tupperware party for this."

Ella Grasso on the political
pomp in Washington.

Because Ella won her seat by a slim margin, her Congressional committee assignments would be crucial to maintaining support. A master at monitoring changing political currents and aware of the strong concern in her district over widespread unemployment and the status of returning Vietnam veterans, she requested appointments to the House Committees on Education and Labor and on Veterans' Affairs. House Speaker, Carl Albert, who knew John Bailey and remembered the promise he had made to Mrs. Grasso at the 1964 national convention, put her on both committees, unheard-of recognition for a first-term legislator.

Despite this seemingly auspicious start, Mrs. Grasso found her life at the Capitol to be dramatically different from that which she had been accustomed to in Hartford. Since the early fifties, at least twenty percent of the legislators in the Connecticut General Assembly had been women. In the 92nd Congress, only fifteen in four hundred and thirty-five Representatives, or, about three percent, were women. In her freshman class of first-term female legislators, the other two women were Democrats—Bella Abzug of New York and Louise Day Hicks of Massachusetts. By their own admission, the three women shared "middle age, motherhood, and overweight." Ella quickly learned that few of her female colleagues, even those with longer tenure, held strong leadership positions in the House, because they were routinely assigned to less powerful committees. Out of the fifteen women that session, four were assigned to Education and Labor. But female members were over-represented on this committee probably because, as one *Courant* report noted:

> It is a panel that has listened closely to its women members in the past. The ladies frequently know more about education than their male colleagues.

Still, none of the four women on that committee were ranking members or chaired its subcommittees. On the Veterans' Affairs Committee, she was the only woman member.

After seventeen years among the elite of the state party leadership, moreover, she realized that she was now part of the rank and file of the House. She attended the meetings for freshmen legislators that she was used to running at home. She served on study groups and task forces similar to those she had been used to leading. Now she was expected to take orders rather than give them and speak when spoken to. Accustomed to authority, power and influence, Mrs. Grasso lashed out against the seniority system where tenure determined leadership. The first freshman in that session to "take a whack" at this long established practice, she told the folks at home that she favored a system where the Chairmen were elected to committees "on the basis of intelligence and leadership." She felt that the party must allow "all the qualities of intelligence and vigor in the House Democratic membership to have full effect."

Her path to power thus thwarted by Committee structure, she soon learned that another of her characteristic methods of gaining influence was unusable. Unable to win favor among the Democratic leadership through committee work because of the seniority system, Mrs. Grasso found she could not attach herself to the most powerful party members—she could not "travel on the inside track" as she had at home with John Bailey. House leader Carl Albert, though impressed by her talents, did not bring her into his entourage. Similarly, Tip O'Neill, another Democratic leader with whom Ella made friends— either because he was not as progressive in his attitudes about women as John Bailey had been or because he did not feel Ella's abilities merited elevated stature—also did not promote Mrs. Grasso within the party.

Nevertheless, Mrs. Grasso attempted early in her first term to stage a coup, which, if successful, would not only give the Democrats dollars to dole out for social services in their districts but also give her increased influence in the House. She and Bill Cotter, another Connecticut Representative, began a move similar to one in progress in the Senate to help President Nixon's planned freeze of over twelve billion dollars that had already received Congressional approval. Their attempt, touted by the *Courant* as the "best political donneybrook of the current session," proved unsuccessful.

After that failure, Mrs. Grasso resigned herself to becoming a member of the rank and file. Unhappy with the slow mobility in the House, Mrs. Grasso noted:

> I can be a gadfly here. But you can't make a long-term career
> out of Congress at age fifty.

Representative Grasso recognized that it would be decades before she could enter the powerful inner circle she had been a part of in Connecticut, so she again set her sights on the statehouse. With that as her ultimate goal, she focused her attention on "bringing home the bacon" for her district and did not attempt to spend further energy amassing a power base in Washington.

Though she abandoned her quest for power within the Congressional leadership, Mrs. Grasso did not ignore the opportunity to win influence in other spheres. As Bailey and Ribicoff had heightened their power by supporting John F. Kennedy early in his career, Ella attempted to attach herself to a promising Presidential nominee. Before Bailey made his decision, Mrs. Grasso came out for Edmund Muskie, a moderate Democrat from Maine. Ella felt that Muskie, like many of the candidates Bailey had successfully backed, including John F. Kennedy, was the definitive middle candidate who could draw broad-base support from the large number of voters who were alienated by McGovern's liberal stands. Muskie sought Mrs. Grasso's help because he wanted to be identified with her advocacy of social issues and hoped, once he had secured her support, he would also gain former national Chairman Bailey's backing. Though Ella's endorsement contributed significantly to Muskie's cause, he did not win the nomination at the national convention.

Ella's style in committee and on the House floor could be best described as "quiet." She rose to speak only occasionally. When she did, it was to comment on legislation affecting her district or relating to her interest in issues relating to the elderly, the handicapped, the mentally retarded, or consumer protection.

That Ella was unhappy during her short tenure at the Capitol was common knowledge among her close associates. She sorely missed her husband Tom, her children, and her parents who remained in Windsor Locks. A doting wife, mother, and daughter, she called home every day. Although after her long work days she sometimes had dinner with party leader Tip O'Neill and other members of the Massachusetts delegation, Ella did not involve herself in the Capitol Hill cocktail and dinner circuit. She preferred to spend her week day evenings quietly in her Potomac Plaza apartment. Afflicted by an ear disorder, Ella did not feel physically well during her stay in Washington. Since her condition made walking difficult, Ella could not move about easily on Capitol Hill. Her fear of escalators further restricted her mobility for she refused to use them, choosing instead to struggle up the long flights of stairs that connected the Congressional office buildings with the Capitol. As a result, she spent long hours in committee rooms doing work brought there by her aides.

Ella also came to detest the weekly commute to her district. The flights she took from Washington's National Airport to Bradley on what she called "Agony Airlines" were overcrowded and unreliable. When weather conditions at Bradley prohibited smaller planes from landing, she had to spend several hours in a Providence airport, while her husband, Tom, waited patiently at the Windsor Locks terminal.

Despite these personal difficulties, Ella worked hard for her district. Given the high levels of unemployment, which reached twenty-five percent in one of her larger industrial towns, Mrs. Grasso focused her efforts on creating jobs. She introduced a bill to control importation of ball bearings, a practice that had had serious consequences for the towns of New Britain and Bristol, both major manufacturers of machine parts. She pressed successfully for industrial park grants for the towns of Plymouth and Bristol. As a conferee on the Emergency Employment Act of 1971, she worked to bring six hundred jobs to her constituents.

On the Veterans' Affairs Committee, she helped bring small gains to veterans of the Vietnam conflict and other wars. She worked on a House-passed bill to authorize a treatment and rehabilitation program for servicemen and veterans suffering from drug addiction. Though her bill to raise educational benefits for veterans to $277 per month didn't get through, it did help assure House passage of a bill that raised benefits to $200, representing an improvement over the existing system.

Ella's activities in committee and on the floor of Congress earned her the label of a "moderate-liberal." Mrs. Grasso's finely-tuned sense of political currents in her district with its large blocks of blue-collar, ethnic voters and numerous factories that turned out defense materials kept her traveling on the middle road. She tended to be moderate on controversial issues and liberal on non-controversial ones, making clear her intention to avoid alienating large segments of her constituents. Her hedging is strongly evident in her stand on the Vietnam conflict. Though Mrs. Grasso complained that the greatest omission of the 92nd Congress was its "failure to establish a cutoff date for troops," she did not rise once on the floor to support or propose measures to end the war. Although she did give her support on two key end-of-war proposals and called for a full accounting of all MIA's, she failed to show up for two other major end-the-war votes in 1971. One of these was a measure which would have restricted U.S. aid to Indochina after December 31, 1971. The other was an amendment which would have prohibited the use of American aid in Indochina after June 1, 1972 provided that prisoners of war were released sixty days earlier. Ella's silence allowed her to avoid incurring Bailey's wrath and a radical image. Her voting record could be used to show workers in the weapon factories that she supported the defense industry as well as to show anti-war liberals that she sympathized with their cause.

Mrs. Grasso's stand on women's issues also illustrated how she skillfully manipulated her position so she could simultaneously identify and disassociate herself with a popular cause. Her personal beliefs and heavy majority of Catholics in her district led her to oppose abortion. She did not show up for the vote on a controversial child-care bill. Ella's strong support for equality in the workplace and in education, however, brought her a rating slightly above average from the Women's Lobby, a group supporting legislation to benefit women. Her efforts on the Education and Labor Committee to secure equal access for women to both universities and technical training programs prevented harsh attacks from feminist groups. Further, since Ella's personal political success strongly aided the cause of women generally, feminist organizations were almost forced to support her. The Women's Political Caucus, although it criticized Ella's stand on abortion and her mediocre Congressional voting record on women's issues, later endorsed her candidacy for governor. In the end, she won the backing from feminists who found it hard to ignore her position in politics and from Catholics who opposed abortion.

Ella Grasso did, however, give her unqualified support to legislation in relatively non-controversial areas. She continued her advocacy for bettering conditions for the young, the elderly, the handicapped, the mentally retarded and consumers. Her support came in the form of votes for increased funding to programs in these areas and in an occasional speech delivered on the floor. Nor did she neglect health and education. She helped pass the Conquest of Cancer Act. Her consistent work in these areas brought her high ratings from the liberal interest group, Americans for Democratic Action. This favorable score kept her friends in labor, liberal, and intellectual circles.

Ella's short career in Congress, like her longer tenure as Secretary of State, provided her with the opportunity to simply amass greater political capital. In a position not always closely monitored by both the press or the public, she could concentrate on pleasing special interest groups through her committee work as well as hedge on, or avoid altogether, issues that might alienate her supporters. In addition, as a member of Congress, Ella could count on the largely favorable media attention usually given to U. S. Representatives. And, she could use the tools of her office to increase her personal contact and rapport with constituents.

In Connecticut, Ella's district office provided strong constituent service. Mrs. Grasso, committed to open government since her days in the League of Women Voters, innovated a system for freer communication between citizens and government officials. She pioneered a no-toll line believing it was absurd that constituents could "make free motel reservations on a no-toll line" but could not call their own Congressional Representitive without charge. The telephone—with the inevitable name of "Ellaphone" formed the focus of Mrs. Grasso's district office in New Britain. Congress members in Connecticut and other states quickly copied her idea. Another practice she initiated which was widely copied by her Congressional colleagues was her holding of "office hours" in the district. Ella's constituents could not only talk to her on the telephone but they could also see her in person. On well-publicized dates, she traveled to different cities and towns to talk to residents. This effort, with its roots in her traveling activities as Secretary of State and in her platform hearings as the chief drafter of the Party programs, proved equally successful, again gaining her publicity and support.

A team of reviewers from the Ralph Nader Congress Project reported that by the end of her first term, Mrs. Grasso had "not proven herself to be a 'superwoman.'" The Emergency Employment Act she worked for did not provide the jobs it promised in that session because of Nixon's freeze. Unemployment remained a critical problem in her district. Five thousand workers in New Britain, 3800 in Bristol, and 3,600 in Torrington were without jobs. And though they praised Ella's efforts in the area of constituent service, the team also noted that Mrs. Grasso had not drafted much legislation.

The voters apparently made a less critical assessment, reelecting her with a sixty percent margin despite Nixon's overwhelming victory and the striking gains made by Republicans in the state's congressional

delegation. Republican Bob Steele won in the second district. Mc-
Kinney was reelected in the first district. Sarasin upset the Democratic
incumbent, Monagan, in the fifth. Cotter and Giamo, both popular
Democrats, did not receive the large pluralities they had once drawn in
their districts. In the sixth, however, while Democratic presidential
candidate lost by almost 50,000 votes, Ella won reelection by almost
40,000 votes. By scoring the most impressive Congressional victory,
Mrs. Grasso clearly strengthened her claim to higher state office.

After the Republican deluge in 1970 and 1972, Bailey faced the
challenge of putting together a winning party ticket for the 1974 gubernatorial race. That year his choices appeared limited. John Dempsey
was adamant about his retirement from politics. Ribicoff was enjoying
immense power and popularity in the U.S. Senate. D'Addario had not
shown that he could draw substantial statewide support. Dodd had died
of a heart attack shortly after he lost his bid for the party's gubernatorial
nomination in 1970. Only two on Bailey's ticket had survived the
Republican landslide: Attorney General Killian and Secretary of State
Gloria Schaffer. Though Schaffer had replaced Ella as the party's top
vote-getter, she did not have Mrs. Grasso's experience and exposure at
the state and national levels. Though Killian also lacked Grasso's long
experience and visibility in public office, he had spent many years
involved in Hartford city politics where Bailey had received his political tutelage under T. J. Spellacy. Yet Mrs. Grasso, a proven vote-
getter, represented a risk. No state had ever elected to the governorship a woman who had not been preceded by her husband. Unable to
make a decision, Bailey followed his familiar strategy—to wait and see.

When Mrs. Grasso returned to Washington for the 93rd session, she
had reason to belive it would be her last. Soon after her reelection,
political observers started to speculate about whether or not Ella could
win the gubernatorial nomination in 1974. Throughout the spring
after her swearing-in, Hartford political writers weighed Mrs. Grasso's
chances. In an April column called "Can a Woman Get Elected
Governor?", Jack Zaiman answered the question he posed in the
affirmative. Pointing to each of Ella's electoral successes, he held out
her nomination and election as strong possibilities. The publishers of
Connecticut Magazine agreed. A professional poll they commissioned

which was released in July tested the strength of the two top Demo-cratic candidates against the incumbent governor, Meskill. Gloria Schaffer came out one percentage point behind the governor. In a contest between Grasso and Meskill, however, the poll showed Mrs. Grasso would run ahead of Meskill by a substantial margin of over ten percentage points. Two other state polls confirmed these results. By the end of the summer, it appeared that a woman could run and win. The woman was to be Ella Grasso.

Chapter Seven

WINNING BIG
1974

*"I keep my campaign promises, but I
never promised to wear stockings."*

Ella Grasso on the 1974
gubernatorial campaign.

In the fall of 1973, Boss Bailey brought his cigar box and ballots around the state. He asked his town party leaders the familiar fourth-year question: "Whadd'ya hear about the governorship?" At a Democratic State Central Committee meeting held later that autumn he posed the same question. All but one of the members present answered: "Ella Grasso."

Ella Grasso was not the only candidate Bailey had been considering. Earlier in the year, Homer Babbidge, former President of the University of Connecticut, had told the Chairman that he was interested in the nomination. The first to announce his candidacy, Babbidge had been traveling around the state, following Bailey's advice to "go around and see people" in an attempt to prove he could garner grass roots support. Frank Zullo, former mayor of Norwalk, also declared his intention to run and had begun making the rounds at Democratic gatherings. There was talk, too, that Attorney General Killian, one of two on the Democratic state ticket to survive the Republican deluge of

1970, planned to enter the race. Throughout 1973, however, Representative Grasso remained publicly silent about her candidacy, as was her custom. To Bailey and others who knew her, it was clear that she wanted to come back to Connecticut and she wanted to be governor.

The Chairman and the state's senior senator, Abraham Ribicoff, stayed scrupulously neutral while potential candidates jockeyed for an early lead. Even when the field narrowed to a choice between Grasso and Killian, Nick Carbone in Hartford and Arthur Barbieri in New Haven and other party leaders in big cities followed suit and refused to commit themselves. They waited for Bailey to decide.

The choice between Grasso and Killian was probably the most difficult decision John Bailey ever had to make. Over the years, he had guided both of their political careers. He had listened to their advice and counsel on matters in the General Assembly and in the Party. On the one hand, Killian's Irish name and background could certainly make him a strong candidate, given the long history of success enjoyed by Irish politicians in the state's high offices. Mim D'Addario's electoral demise in 1970, led Bailey to doubt the ability of Italo-Americans to win the governorship. But on the other hand, Ella's Italian surname and sex had not hindered and may have even contributed to her unparalleled electoral success. In the last two elections, Killian had shown strong state-wide support, but John Bailey remained unconvinced, acknowledging that Ella had "helped put this whole thing together for the Democrats back in '53." His reminder recalled the days when the two of them had fashioned a victory for Ribicoff and continued to maintain the governor's momentum by calling the shots in the Legislature.

Some facets of the Chairman's relationship with Killian, however, did not work in Ella's favor. They had first met when Hartford Mayor T. J. Spellacy sent young Bailey to congratulate Killian, the star football player for his winning touchdown in a city championship. Killian, like Bailey, got his start in Hartford city politics. Although their two families were well acquainted, it was not until the mid-sixties that a strong friendship developed between them. Bailey, who had worked with Ella on the Ribicoff campaign in the early '50s, was personally closer to Killian than Grasso. Some even said the Chairman had made a personal promise to Attorney General Killian to support him for governor. Still, Bailey continued his "wait and see" policy, watching the polls and listening to people.

As 1973 grew to a close, the picture began to look brighter for the Democrats after a devastating storm caused Governor Meskill's reputation to suffer significantly. When the storm hit the state, the governor got the National Guard to clear away the snow, put his chief aide in charge, and then left for Vermont on a ski trip. Needless to say, the image of Meskill enjoying a vacation with his family while the rest of the state remained paralyzed because of the heavy snow, infuriated his Connecticut constituency. Despite the fact that Meskill had turned a fiscal surplus for three consecutive years, his popularity plunged as a result of his handling of the storm.

Shortly after Meskill's blunder, when the threat of a gubernatorial race against an incumbent had lessened considerably, Killian announced his candidacy, followed by Frank Zullo. Three days afterward, on January 18, several hundred people braved the icy weather to watch Ella give her announcement speech in Windsor Locks. There she also named William O'Neill, a state legislator and bar owner from East Hampton, as her campaign chairperson.

Ella's selection of O'Neill as her campaign manager had strong political implications. It told Bailey she still wanted to run on the insider's track. O'Neill, a popular figure in the Party, had the perfect qualifications according to the Boss's bible. Firstly, he was of Irish decent, historically a crucial criterion for success in Connecticut politics. Since the candidate herself was not, the next best thing was to surround herself with those of Irish background. Secondly, he was from a small town; because the state was comprised of scores of those towns, it made sense to choose a candidate who could consolidate support for her in those towns. Finally, O'Neill was regarded as an insider in the Democratic House operation at the Legislature. Because Ella wanted Bailey's help and encouragement, she needed to show him that she found his organization valuable.

Grasso's efforts to prove to Bailey she could win substantial support went beyond the symbolic. In February of 1974, negotiations with the New Haven Party yielded endorsements from New Haven boss Arthur

Barbieri and Mayor Bart Guida. Endorsements followed from the city of Stamford. Anxious, for good reason, Killian attacked the Chairman for not giving "the type of leadership" that was needed and said his tactics would force a primary. Grasso then praised Bailey in the press for his "fair and equitable policy." In March, she and her captains leveled what would be a fatal blow for Killian's candidacy. One of her key supporters, a "street-fighting" liberal, Nick Carbone, gained control of the Hartford Town Committee. Two weeks later, he announced his endorsement of Ella and said that a majority of the city's delegation would follow his lead. Killian had no choice but to call a primary in order to win the votes of the Hartford delegation—the largest block of convention delegates in the state.

The political capital Ella had accumulated over her years in the Secretary of State's office and in Congress became evident as soon as Killian called for a primary. In a preconvention blitz, important Democratic leaders and powerful interest groups across the state began to endorse her. She had already won the big cities to her side. Rarely a day went by when mayors or town committees of smaller towns did not register their support. Labor, liberal, and education groups eagerly climbed aboard the Grasso bandwagon.

On May 23, Grasso scored one of the most stunning political coups in her career. She defeated Killian in his hometown of Hartford by nearly 2,000 votes, 6,481 to 4,562. In that race, Mrs. Grasso had proven her colors and Bailey began to put together a state ticket to run with her. Now the Chairman's skills as a compromiser and a party leader would be tested, for he wanted to unify the Party by bringing Killian back into the fold. After six weeks of negotiations, Killian agreed not to attempt a statewide primary and to run instead with Ella for Lieutenant Governor. Some speculated that Bailey had promised him a nomination to the governorship in '78, while others felt Killian needed to play second fiddle to Ella to save his career.

Grasso agreed to the arrangement despite her intense personal distaste for Killian, who had dared to opposed her, because she knew her acceptance was a requisite for Bailey's help in the coming race. She needed Bailey's strong state-wide organization and wanted to be identified with his moderate-liberal politics. The younger, more liberal members of the party, led by Nick Carbone, criticized Ella sharply for her retreat to the "Old Guard" embodied in her choice of Bob Killian as a running mate. Carbone and his allies lobbied to bring new blood into the party, hoping to nominate Bill O'Neill or James Kennelly, whom they felt would be more liberal and independent as a lieutenant governor. Carbone insisted also on supporting a distinguished young attorney, Sanford Cloud, over the popular party choice, Hank Parker, for Treasurer. Ella remained adamant, clinging tightly to the "Old Guard" by backing Bailey's choices. The convention proved anticlimatic for Bailey had done his work well. The 1,207 delegates nominated Mrs. Grasso and Mr. Killian unanimously. Parker easily trounced Cloud.

While Ella worked to identify herself with the established wing of the party, her Republican opponent, U. S. Representative Robert Steele, Jr., tried to disassociate himself from his Party's Old Guard. Steele, the two-term Congress member from the second district in central Connecticut and son of the popular Connecticut radio personality, Robert Steele, Sr., had defeated the party man, Mayor Panuzio of Bridgeport to win the gubernatorial nomination. An advocate of what he called "the new Politics," Steele then moved to unseat the longtime Republican Chairman, Brian Gaffney. Afraid of what the repercussions of the Watergate hearings might mean for his candidacy, Steele attempted from the start to portray himself as a leader who would remake and reinvigorate the Republican Party. Steele went out of his way to remove himself from the Republican fray. His advertisements rarely mentioned that he was a Republican. His small group of campaign workers were not party regulars. Unlike his predecessors in the Party and more like his Democratic counterparts, he refused to take contributions of over one hundred dollars, declaring his intention to rid of "big money" and "the old politics."

Ella and every other Democratic candidate in the state took full advantage of the Watergate wrong-doings. She proposed stronger freedom of information laws and promised "open" government. One did not need to look at the fine print of Ella's campaign literature to know she was a Democrat. Her large organization contained a lot of "Killian people" and party regulars from John Bailey's statewide machine swelled its ranks. Notably, some of Ella's colleagues from the campaign to elect Ribicoff as governor in 1954, like Herman Wolf and Alexander Goldfarb, now played important roles in her organization. Despite the renewed stigma that Watergate had attached to long party service, Ella appealed to the large numbers of moderate Democrats in the state by frequently reminding them that she had "paid her dues." Further, she benefited from the fact that because she was a woman, she was not perceived by the public as a "party hack."

The Watergate scandal aside, other political currents profoundly influenced the actions of both candidates during the campaign. Most important, perhaps, was organized feminism which had expanded its scope and direction in the early seventies. A new, more moderate strain, in contrast to the militants and radicals that had characterized the late sixties, emerged in the women's movement and spurred the development of three national, middle-of-the-road political action groups. The first of these, the National Organization for Women, actually established by Betty Friedan and her supporters in 1966, aimed to pressure the government on behalf of women in the same way civil rights organizations functioned for blacks. In 1970 academic and professional women started the Women's Equity Action League in an effort to end discrimination in employment, education, and taxation through legal means. To pioneer another frontier—politics—Bella Abzug and Shirley Chisholm founded the National Women's Political Caucus to help elect female candidates and to force political parties to consider women's issues.

In many respects, the political realm did form the final frontier for women. Though inequalities in employment and educational opportunities had by no means been eradicated, the gaps in pay and school admissions appeared to be narrowing in the late sixties and early seventies. Legal victories for women in discrimination cases came more frequently than in past decades. The picture of women in politics, however, was a dismal one. Percentages of women holding elected office remained negligible and had not changed perceptibly in the last century. Since women received the vote in 1920, only sixty-five females had been elected to the House of Representatives, comprising a total of two percent of that body's membership. Almost all of these women were widows of former Congress members before they ran for office. Almost half of them served one term or less. Since the turn of the century only two women had served as cabinet members. President Franklin D. Roosevelt had appointed Frances Perkins as Secretary of the Department of Labor and President Dwight D. Eisenhower had appointed Ovetta Culp Hobby as Secretary of the Department of Health, Education, and Welfare. Equally dismal was the situation at the state level. Between 1900 and 1970, only three female governors, all of whom had been preceded by their husbands, were elected. One woman had served as an attorney general and three had served as lieutenant governors. Women had, however, make inroads in the position of secretary of state. After the May primary, when Ella's nomination became a foregone conclusion, the national media turned their attention to the Connecticut gubernatorial race. If Ella Grasso won the election, as indeed Bailey's backing strongly indicated that she might, she would be the first woman governor elected in her own right. Her victory would represent an historic moment for the women's movement. Or, as *Connecticut Magazine* noted in the rhetoric of the time:

> If she (Grasso) gets the job she has her heart set on, Ella Grasso will have conquered the oldest bastion of male chauvinism in Connecticut: the governor's office. Since 1639, that office has been totally oblivious to women's liberation, its 335-year history an unbroken succession of 83 male incumbants.

Other National magazines representing a gamut of political and social viewpoints took note of Ella's unique position. *Time, Newsweek, U.S. News and World report, Ms., Commonweal, People, Catholic Digest,* and *Ladies' Home Journal* wrote many features on Ella's candidacy. In the advent of the seventies's feminism, rooted in a broader social base, the Grasso/Steele race became a national media event. It even drew international attention. Given strong possibility that Connecticut would elect its first Italo-American governor, the Italian press came to the Capitol in Hartford to photograph Ella Rosa Giovanni Tambussi Grasso.

Ella Grasso, whose political style was characterized by caution and whose career had been built on compromise rather than controversy, "soft-peddled"(sic) the feminist issue. One reason for her unemotional attitude toward the "symbolic" magnitude of becoming the first female governor not preceded by her husband, can be ground in her desire to remain detached from the feminist cause to avoid alienating large segments of Catholic and working-class voters. This strategy, similar to the one she had followed on the abortion issue during her Congressional term, allowed her to play both sides. She kept the support of a majority of the electorate by not participating formally in the women's movement. At the same time, though she offered little in the way of commitment on issues, she held out her political success to appeal to feminists. As Fredrica Wechsler, the political action coordinator of the National Women's Political Caucus, which ultimately endorsed Mrs. Grasso, pointed out:

> She's (Grasso) not what you'd call an out-and-out feminist, but willy-nilly, any woman who is out there making it is part of the women's movement and will serve as an example to other women.

In the end, she got the support of non-feminists and feminists alike.

Ella's relative silence on the issue of gender, as *Connecticut Magazine* suggested, had much to do with the fact that for two decades she had proved herself to be an upwardly mobile politician, winning her laurels from within an organization dominated by men. She had achieved her position without making waves and had advised Connecticut feminists supporting the equal rights amendment to do the same, warning that "student voices" could accomplish only alienation.

Though Ella Grasso never went out of her way to support feminism, she did not oppose it. Nor did she avoid questions about her personal convictions. Over the course of the campaign, she developed a set of stock answers to queries about feminism and the issue of gender. They ran:

> I would like to think that I am a feminist in the sense that I would support vigorously the fight against discrimination to assure equality of life under the law.

People aren't looking at me as a woman; they're looking at
my stands on major issues. My experience in government has
earned me a shot at the office of governor. I've paid my dues.

The governorship is neither a man's nor woman's work. I
see it as a people's job.

She sought a "people's job" and she called herself the "people's
candidate." It is striking that this catch phrase evoked those themes
similar to those created by Bailey's organization in Ribicoff 's campaign
for the governorship in 1954. Ella successfully attempted, as Abe had
done, to convince the voters of her worth by portraying herself as an
ethnic girl from a poor-working-class family who had attained success
through hard work. Part truth, part myth, Grasso and her colleagues
schooled in Bailey's politics knew this image had particular appeal for
the ethnic and working-class voters that comprised the majority of the
state's population. Ribicoff 's electoral success attested to the strength of
this strategy.

Another similarity existed between Grasso's and Ribicoff 's gubernatorial campaigns. Twenty years before, Bailey and the leadership of
Ribicoff 's campaign organization had decided to "forget about issues"
and "let the candidate's personality stand above all." In her 1974 effort, Grasso used the same technique, choosing to rely heavily on her
widespread popularity across the state. Her buttons and bumperstickers
read simply: "Ella," though John Bailey jokingly criticized this tack :
"Whadd'ya gonna do when the voters don't see 'Ella' on the ballot?"
Her general campaign pamphlet entitled "We All Win With Ella: the
Proven Vote Getter" did not mention a single issue. Rather, it cited
her past electoral victories, cataloguing her large pluralities in '62, '70,
and '72 proclaiming: "Ella Grasso led the ticket twice before; she'll lead
it to victory again in '74." Her campaign literature made her seem
more like a party leader than a candidate, for in it her major concern
was clear: to win and to win big.

The national media, especially the news magazines, reinforced the
image Ella was promoting in her Connecticut campaign. Even the
briefest articles on the Grasso-Steele race did not fail to mention her
Italian parentage and her childhood in Windsor Locks. *Newsweek's*

version, somewhat romantically overplaying the Tambussi's poverty, was typical:

> Both her (Grasso's) parents were grammar school dropouts who came (in) steerage from Italy to the small milltown in Windsor Locks, Connecticut. Grasso, an only child, won a scholarship to the exclusive Chaffee school while Papa Tambussi worked fourteen hour shifts in a bakery to pay for her transportation, lunch, and books.

Writers at *Time* and *Newsweek* also lauded her intellectual achievements at Mount Holyoke while praising her down-to-earth manner. In a piece called "Grasso: Piedmont Spoken Here," the *Time* author noted:

> A Phi Beta Kappa graduate from Mount Holyoke, Grasso speaks the language of the classroom as easily as she does the piedmont dialect of Italy on the front porch.

Grasso benefited immeasurably from these portrayals because they associated her with the American Dream and strengthened the electorate's ethnic pride.

Ella's "folksy" campaign style further enhanced this major theme for she proved most effective at gatherings of working-class and ethnic people. She felt comfortable at factory gates and union meetings. She enjoyed speaking Italian with immigrants and Italo-Americans. Ella's warm manner and casual style of dress put people at ease. Her twenty years of travel around Connecticut in various capacities made her familiar with its many urban and rural communities. Wherever Ella went, she knew people and called them by name.

At large campaign gatherings, Steele appeared ill at ease and had difficulty greeting his supporters. After countless clambakes and chicken dinners, communion breakfasts and cake sales, Ella had become a master at working the crowds and pressing the flesh. One sunny Sunday in August of 1974, Ella delivered a performance that was envied among the most talented of Connecticut's politicians. When she arrived at Hammonassett, one of the state's largest public beaches, Ella kicked off her espadrilles and rolled up her white polyester pants to her ankles. Her glasses were pushed up off her forehead, Bailey-style. Rather than seeking out groups of people on the beach and greeting them, Ella chose simply to walk along the water. As she moved casually past the volleyball nets and sand castles at the water's edge, some of the older children recognized her. As she walked further along the shore, more children and their curious parents followed. Before she had gone several hundred yards, more than a hundred people had assembled behind her. Seemingly unaware of the mass attention, Ella continued to splash her feet softly in the water and to talk in conversational tones with both personal acquaintances and those who approached her. When she left after a few hours, someone in the crowd said that "Everybody was feeling pretty good."

Mr. Steele suffered in comparison to his opponent in the national media. Attention focused on Ella because of her unique background and her chance to become the first female governor elected in her own right. Nearly all of the articles about the Connecticut gubernatorial contest barely mentioned Steele's name. In their full-page stories on the race, *Time* and *Newsweek* referred to Steele by name not more than twice. Mr. Steele's campaign style also paled in comparison to his experienced opponent. The young Representative appeared noticeably uncomfortable with people of different age and income groups. He couldn't speak Italian. Nor did he appear to know many people when he visited the state's towns and cities on his campaign trail.

Some of Steele's woes were exacerbated by the fact that the race was relatively issueless, so that voters had to look at media coverage and campaign style to make their choice. On the two most volatile issues of the campaign agenda—abortion and busing—the two candidates took the same stand. Both opposed abortion because of the large number of Catholic voters in Connecticut. Both opposed school busing, which was highly unpopular in the state, despite the fact that it was law and the winner of the contest would have to enforce it. Both candidates also came out against legalized marijuana and both refused to take a stand on the proposed Route 7 highway project.

Steele, warned by Brian Gaffney, the Republican State Chairman, that Grasso was a non-issue type, attempted to get Ella to commit herself on some hard issues. He struck first with the most difficult question of all for Connecticut politicians—the income tax. Citizens in the state had vehemently opposed such a tax and when a bill proposing a levy on personal incomes passed late in the 1971 legislative session, the uproar was so great that legislators met six weeks later to repeal it. Before the May primary, Grasso evaded the issue by saying that at the present time she did not feel the state needed extra revenue to operate, but when other sources were needed she would consider "all forms of taxation." In the heat of the campaign, however, Steele's opposition to the tax forced her to come out violently against it. Even though she knew Connecticut's financial situation required overhauling, Grasso pledged that if and when income tax ever came to her desk, she would veto it. In opposing the tax, she followed in the footsteps of the other Bailey-trained Democratic Governors, Ribicoff and Dempsey.

Steele's inability to trap his opponent on the income tax and other questions put him increasingly on the offensive. Early on in her campaign, Grasso learned that a chief concern of the voters was the high cost of energy. When Ella quickly jumped on the bandwagon and accused three Connecticut utility companies of overcharging customers by nineteen million dollars in fuel adjustments, Steele called her a demagogue. After Grasso filed a class-action suit against the utilities and pledged to reorganize the Public Utilities Commission, Steele claimed the real issue lay in the regional disparity of oil prices. He retaliated by suing the Federal Energy Administration to force equalization in energy prices. Steele's belated effort to capitalize on the public furor over fuel costs, however, met with failure. The stir over the utilities scandal had added considerably to Grasso's momentum and his case against the Energy Administration remained unresolved on election day.

By the fall of 1974, the Republican camp knew Steele was in trouble. The Party refused to release the results of the professional polls they commissioned. Running scared, Steele moved to attack Ella's program directly. He called her "Spenderella" and charged that her pledge to increase spending in the areas of urban aid, social services, education, and transportation would cost the state an additional four hundred million dollars and could only be financed by an increase in the state's sales tax. His accusations fell on deaf ears. The electorate seemed

convinced of Ella Grasso's famed frugality, which the press had docu-
mented frequently since her days in the General Assembly. Few cars
sported the Republican bumpersticker: "Connecticut Can't Afford A
Governess."

Desperate, Steele resorted to an attack on John Bailey, a traditional
strategy for Republican candidates in dire situations. Two weeks before
the election, Steele charged that Ella had been "hand-picked by her
boss, John Bailey," and that Bailey had been—"quietly and meth-
odically lining his pockets with money that should have gone to the
customers of Hartford Electric Light Company." His charge referred to
a building Bailey had bought from the utility company at a price Steele
believed was too low. Grasso and a Republican colleague of Steele's,
Senator Lowell Weicker, rushed to Bailey's defense. Weicker's sharp
criticism of Steele's tactics only added to the cause of the Democrats.

Though the campaign appeared to be moving smoothly, Ella Grasso
was not without her troubles. As the race drew to a close, Nick
Carbone, at first a vigorous and vocal supporter, and some of his liberal
followers had begun to turn against her because they felt she abandoned
her commitment to aid urban areas. Their disillusionment with her
also stemmed from the fact that they felt she followed Bailey's rules too
closely. Nor could Boss Bailey quell their dissent. The cancer he had
been battling for several years now confined him to a bed in Hartford
Hospital. Ella knew she would soon have to face the inevitable—the
death of her closest advisor and disunity in the ranks of the Democratic
Party.

Another unpleasant undercurrent no doubt gnawed at her. Though
she tried to play down the issue of gender, sex remained a "quiet issue."
Comments about her "messy" hair, her "dowdy" clothes, and "unfashionable" shoes found their way into virtually every news item about
the campaign, while a female political columnist at the *Courant* noted
that Mr. Steele's "polyester suits and white shoes" went unnoticed.
Mr. Steele's camp also coined the catchy phrases: "Ella fella" and
"Spenderalla." Mr. Steele's campaign manager told one journalist at
the *Advoacate* that:

> I personally could never vote for a woman, Democrat or
> Republican. They just don't have the emotional stability. I

mean, what do we do when a woman her has period? Just close down the government?

Yet it was not only the opposition that was at fault. Her own running mate, Mr. Killian, made several blatantly sexist remarks to the press. The candidate for lieutenant governor in an interview published in a June 1974 issue of the weekly *People* magazine said: "What can you say about a woman who doesn't wear stockings?"

Most of these comments, to be sure, did not merit a response. Still, the fact that such remarks probably expressed frustration with her success could not be very comforting, for every day she knew the electorate would be influenced by what they read in newspapers and magazines.

In the end, Boss Bailey had been right in his refusal to "dress Ella up" for the campaign. On November 5, the electorate chose a woman who happened to care little about her appearance. Ella defeated Steele by a huge plurality of over 200,000 votes. This total was second only to the number Ribicoff had received in his 1958 reelection race. Another student of Bailey's, Abe Ribicoff, broke another record in 1974; he won his senate seat with an unprecedented plurality of 300,000 votes. Both of Boss Bailey's star pupils basked in the bright light of brilliant electoral success. They had won and they had won big.

Many factors influenced Ella's impressive victory. To be sure, the extensive national media coverage she received played a role. In the year when the Watergate scandal was prominent in the minds of voters, Ella's party affiliation worked in her favor. Even though Ella was the product of Bailey's organization, because she was a woman, the majority did not perceive her as a "party hack" or a member of the tainted "Old Guard."

There were other subtler reasons for her win. In the 1974 election, the "well-oiled" Bailey Machine produced what would be its last and biggest victory. Under the leadership of its dying commander, the Democratic Party mobilized behind Ella its traditional blocks of support—labor, liberals, ethnics, Catholics, blacks, and urban dwellers. Ella and the organization had rallied these groups behind the ticket by promising increased aid to cities, public transportation, and education as well as by opposing abortion. In order to poll a huge plurality reminiscent of Ribicoff 's landslide in 1958, however, Ella had to make her platform palatable to voters in the politically conservative sections of the state—the small towns and suburban communities bordering New York, both areas that Ribicoff had first begun to tap in 1954. Knowing she could not win the wealthy counties of Litchfield and Fairfield with liberal stands on issues, Ella denounced integration by busing and came out strongly against the income tax. In doing so, she, like Ribicoff, departed from the liberal tradition established by Chester Bowles who had been an ardent advocate of the tax during his term as governor three decades before. By moving the Party toward a more moderate center with her stand on the income tax and other issues, Ella gained significant support from traditionally Republican areas.

Ella's huge win in 1974 did not signal sweeping change in the Connecticut party's platform and strategy. Bailey's organization had amassed great power by advocating a conservative stand on the personal income tax issue. In his first speech of the 1954 campaign given in Greenwich, "the heartland of suburban Fairfield county," Ribicoff registered strong opposition to an income tax and gained crucial votes in that area. During his reelection campaign for the governorship in 1958, he played up the issue and increased his margin of victory in traditionally Republican Fairfield and Litchfield counties to over fifty-six percent, much to the dismay of the opposition party. Some Republican leaders even began to complain that the conservative Ribicoff had stolen one of their most reliable political arguments. One candidate lamented:

> How can you say you're against the tax when all anyone will
> say in reply is that "So is Abe."

By the time Grasso ran for governor in 1974, the strategy had become a tried and true ticket to electoral success. She carried every county in the State. So did Ribicoff. In his bid for his third term in the Senate, he also captured every county by more than fifty-nine percent.

The 1974 election marked the culmination of the efforts of Ella, Abe, and Bailey's organization to win by huge pluralities. Careful construction of a moderate state platform maximized their support among conservative and traditional elements. Their platform was called Democratic, but it could easily have been confused as Republican. On the one hand, they called for aid for expanded social programs. On the other, they opposed abortion, integration by busing and progressive taxation and, therefore, could be construed to oppose women, minorities, and the poor. Their shrewd mix of issues, however, prevented mass alienation of these groups that brought the Party to power after the New Deal. Since the Republican Party in the state offered nothing better, women, blacks, and the urban poor still voted for Bailey's tickets.

The Democratic party managed this delicate balance because it had indeed helped some of the disadvantaged groups in Connecticut. Ella and Abe themselves had led the fight for important and popular liberal causes—consumer protection, civil rights, peace in Vietnam. The social programs created under the Dempsey administration through Ella's "citizen's lobby" were among the best in the country. Still, the party's platform in 1974 represented a less than total commitment to the liberal concern of social equality. Yet given political realities influenced by existing demographic, economic, and social conditions, Bailey's organization did not need to make such a strong commitment to that ideal. Bailey and his captains had derived the proper formula according to those conditions and successfully applied it to win.

Chapter Eight

HARSH REALITIES
1975-1976

*"The time of plenty, the days of
wine and roses are over."*

Hugh Carey, Governor of New York.

The headiness from her huge victory ended quickly. At a private meeting held the day after the election, the governor told the governor-elect that his administration would be leaving a seventy million dollar debt. Ella found the news particularly shocking because in the past months Meskill had been promising he would end his term with a balanced budget. It appeared that the Republican governor, who himself had inherited Dempsey's two hundred and forty-four million dollar deficit, was returning the favor to the Democrats. Soon after Meskill's announcement, a cursory investigation revealed several months of unpaid medical bills in the welfare department as well as other unaccounted expenses which brought the projected deficit to more than two hundred million dollars.

At the meeting with Meskill the day after her election, Ella Grasso saw her political world begin to tumble down around her. Without abundant financial resources she could not provide the new social services she had promised. She could not amass political capital by wooing interest groups because she would have to spend more time and resources on the less popular task of balancing the budget. And she would face inevitable challenges to her reputation as a "caring" and "compassionate" advocate for the disadvantaged—a reputation upon which her previous political and electoral success had been built. Unremedied, the crisis threatened her immense personal popularity.

Though the severe revenue shortfall would soon change not only her program and strategy, but also her style and image, Ella Grasso responded in the interim period with her traditional tactics. Her immediate, and by now almost instinctive reaction to the news of the deficit came in the form of her characteristic displays of frugality. Lacking the power to do much in the way of substantial policy, the governor-elect took several symbolic steps to diminish the state's debt. She told the press that she would not order new stationery for the governor's office until all of Meskill's supply had been used and announced her intention to cross out his name and add her own. After the release, a Hartford printer who felt that even given the hard times Mrs. Grasso was taking things too far, personally donated new gubernatorial letterhead. Still, the public applauded her effort. Later that month, Ella announced that she would forego the use of the luxurious gubernatorial limousine and use her 1971 economy car or a state police cruiser instead.

On the more substantive side of the financial crisis, Ella coped with the situation in the interim period by calling into service a friend and colleague from her days in the Bailey braintrust, George Conkling. She asked Conkling, a former finance and transportation commissioner under Dempsey and then in semi-retirement, to represent her at conferences on the budget with the Meskill administration. Ella put him to work planning a program to remedy the state's financial ills.

Despite his rapidly failing health, John Bailey participated actively in the formation of the Grasso government after the election. Ella visited him at his home or in the hospital almost every day because she needed and wanted his advice on the hundreds of appointments she was called upon to make. There were even rumors manufactured by the press that Bailey left the hospital one day to hand out patronage at the Capitol. During the weeks before her inauguration, the governor-elect and the ailing party leader naturally focused their efforts on the selection of a finance commissioner because of the public concern over the state's fiscal condition. Mrs. Grasso sent the strongest candidates to Hartford Hospital to be interviewed by Mr. Bailey. When Jay Tepper answered "Yes" to the question of whether he could manage the state's finances without an income tax, Grasso and Bailey took the former Ohio finance commissioner on board the Connecticut ship.

Both Bailey and Grasso had been impressed with Tepper's credentials; he had studied economics and had a degree from the Wharton School of Finance. Like Tepper, the other people Ella chose as her close advisors were also young, bright, highly educated and devoted to her. The small circle of aides she brought together resembled the braintrust Bailey formed during his heyday at the Capitol. And almost all of Ella's "palace guard" had been well schooled in Bailey politics.

Nancy Lewinsohn, whom Ella chose as her executive aide, had gone to work as a special assistant for Senator Abe Ribicoff after earning a bachelor's degree from Smith and a master's and a doctorate degree from Harvard. She then had run Ella's congressional office for four years and had helped Bailey direct her second congressional and gubernatorial campaigns. Over the years, Ella had come to value Nancy's abilities and to trust her judgment. Lewinsohn would be the "undisputed boss of the staff" and Ella would rely on her heavily in all policy and personal matters.

Second in command would Aaron Ment, the governor's legal counsel and legislative liaison. Ment, who was forty-one and a graduate of the University of Connecticut and of Boston University Law School, spent six years as an alderman in the big-city Democratic machine in Bridgeport. Since 1967, Ment acted as counsel to a succession of Party speakers and minority leaders in the General Assembly. During his years at the Legislature, he became friends with and gave legal advice to John Bailey.

Ella also signed on Jeff Daniels, a young and experienced journalist, to serve as a special assistant for policy and programs. Daniels would work on broad issue areas such as energy and utility regulation. As a reporter for the *Hartford Times* and several other newspapers, as well as a press aide in Grasso's campaign, Daniels had come to understand the dynamics of Bailey politics. Other key staff members Ella selected were

Press Secretary Larrye deBear, a long-time Connecticut journalist and political analyst; Executive aide John Dempsey, Jr., son of the former governor, who had worked in her Congressional office and on her campaigns; and administrative assistant Charles McCollam, who was a Bailey-trained expert in local politics. With her braintrust assembled and major staff appointments considered, Ella was ready to take command.

Early on the morning of January 8, 1975, Ella Grasso, the governor elect, went to worship with "her people" at St. Mary's Church in Windsor Locks. Friends, neighbors, and well-wishers joined Father Bollea to celebrate Ella's inauguration which would be held in Hartford later that day. One observer noted that the gathering at the Church looked like the crowded "Sunday-at-eight" service. After the mass ended, Ella met more townspeople at a reception held in her honor at the familiar Knights of Columbus Hall. She greeted by name nearly all of the three hundred who had gathered there. For the occasion, Ella wore a blue satin dress made for her by Bice Clemow, a male newspaper editor from West Hartford. Clemow, afraid that Ella would wear something unfashionable for the historic event, insisted on making her inauguration outfit. Ella radiated in the frock despite its rather unflattering color and uneven hemline. When the breakfast was over, Ella led her family and the entourage of press and security people to the town train station where they would catch the 9:50 a.m. train for Hartford. Her widely publicized ride was intended to dramatize the need for a consolidated and improved public transit system.

On the way to the station, Ella chatted in Italian and cautioned reporters not to walk in the streets. As the large group passed by the Doughnut Kettle, a "working-man's diner" in front of the water locks, she waved at the many patrons cheering: "Ella! Ella! Windsor Locks! Windsor Locks!" As they boarded the cars, Ella joked that years ago the conductor never waited for her when she had to catch the morning train to Chaffee. The crowd waved and cheered again. She was still holding a single red rose given to her at the mass earlier in the day. In the midst of this scene with Ella, the homely child of immigrant parents clad in homemade clothes and leaving for the big city, the myth created by the media appeared to mesh with reality for a warm moment.

Mrs. Grasso's virtuoso performance prior to her inaugural speech suggested that of an ethnic machine-style politician, but her address reflected that of a tough-minded fiscal manager. Though she did not appear to wholly abandon the political style she had developed in the Bailey years, the tone of her inaugural did not coincide with previous speeches given in the Party's big-spending heyday. She omitted the rhetoric which one journalist called "Kennedyish" and replaced it with the straight talk Hugh Carey had adopted in response to his state's failing finances. In her first words as governor, Ella recalled the beginning of her political career and spoke fondly of Windsor Locks. She indulged in this recollection only briefly, turning immediately and abruptly to Connecticut's unfavorable economic position:

> The situation is serious. The long-range prospects are not encouraging. Our course is clear.

With this introduction, she stated her goal of "efficient, compassionate, and humane" government and outlined her plan to overcome the projected two hundred million dollar deficit.

"Efficiency" meant restructuring. As chief executive, Ella, the ardent advocate of government reorganization, finally had not only compelling reason but also authority to initiate such a program. The Mount Holyoke economics scholar promised that under her administration every agency would be evaluated to ensure that every tax dollar met the "test of maximum effective use." Two departments—public works and welfare—she noted needed major overhauling. In order to maximize her ability to solve fiscal problems and to revitalize the state's economy, Mrs. Grasso announced her intention to bring the state's Council of Economic Advisors Closer to the governor's office.

More importantly, efficiency meant major cuts in capital investment and in social programs. The "belt-tightening" she referred to would occur in the human service areas she had lobbied so strenuously for in her many years at the Capitol.

The governor struck an uncomfortable balance between the "efficient" and the "compassionate" and "humane." In her half-hour address, she did not mention the plight of the cities. The revenue-sharing which she had promised to earmark for urban aid would obviously now be used to pay the state's creditors. In the area of transportation, she spoke only of "consolidation" and "unification" rather than of expansion and development. And on the subject of education, her comments were vague—she pledged to "work to develop the means to better our children's world." Ella, the "compassionate" candidate that "cared," had little to say on behalf of the disadvantaged. Though she promised she would not forget the elderly, the handicapped, the ill and the veterans, she could offer almost nothing in the way of programs. To complete her seemingly sweeping dismissal of the groups that had strongly supported her, she did not even mention her vision for women or minorities.

Lack of money to expand and initiate social programs forced Ella to make reform the centerpiece of her first-year plan. She reiterated her commitment to open government. "Right-to-know" laws would be rewritten and strengthened. She announced that she would require all of her top level appointees to disclose their income and assets and asked all of her other state officers and Assembly members to do the same. She promised that public hearings would be held before serious budgetary and tax decisions were made. The governor called for changes in the state's leasing, bonding, and judicial selection practices, all of which had come under increasing scrutiny during Meskill's administration. Although Ella did not promise to refund utility consumers for overcharges, she did voice her support for the creation of a Public Utilities Control Authority to replace the ineffective Public Utilities Commission.

Even though Ella did not propose many new programs and ignored large segments in her constituency, she received hearty applause, more than twenty-seven times during her short speech. Indeed, many of her colleagues who had joined the new governor in the Hall of the House that day not only believed in her strategies to balance the budget, but also shared her moderate position on a number of substantive issues. This was most obviously reflected in the single standing ovation she got when she vowed that she would bring the state's finances in the black without "recourse to a personal income tax." The Party's commitment to maintaining the status quo was further evidenced in one of the votes taken later in the day immediately after the inaugural address. The large Democratic majority easily defeated a measure which would have made the process of judicial selection more open and less influenced by partisan considerations. It would have ended secret votes on confirmation of judges.

Ella was not the only Democrat to triumph in a virtuoso performance that day. While she led a parade of people in a march to the inaugural ceremonies from Hartford's Union Station, Mr. Baily prepared to emerge from his hospital room for the day's festivities. The dying Democratic Chairman could not be kept away from the celebration of the sixth and last gubernatorial victory of his career. Wan and pale, but happy, the Boss galantly presided at the Party's events. One political writer called his presence "bittersweet"—the Democratic family was briefly re-united, yet they knew it would not be long before they would lose their father. Their mother expressed her appreciation to the press: "I'm honored and proud that my good friend and political mentor was able to share this day with me."

Just ten days after the huge Democratic majority in the House voted to defeat a measure to open up the judicial process, the Party appeared to break another of its major campaign platform promises. Ella announced at a meeting of the state's mayors that she would no longer be able to make good on her pledge to increase the amount of federal revenue sharing funds given to cities from six million dollars to twenty-five million dollars for property tax relief. She even went so far as to suggest that "harsh realities" might prevent her from sending the six million dollars in earmarked funds to the municipalities. Some of the mayors offered to help sell an increase in the already burdensome sales tax to diminish the deficit. Ella, however, refused, not because she opposed the regressiveness of the tax, but because she felt she could not afford to do so politically. Her withdrawal of her commitment to urban aid fanned the flames of criticism from the party's liberal wing led by Nick Carbone and from her Republican opponents.

Ella Grasso did intend to make good on her promise to put the state on sound fiscal footing without resorting to a personal income tax. The governor's commissioners, journalists speculated, reflected Ella's strong desire to avoid the tax. Her small staff comprised of young, bright, energetic individuals contrasted sharply with her agency directors who were comparatively older and less creative. Her critics argued that she deliberately chose "mediocre" bureaucrats as department heads rather than "bright activists" who would spend their time creating new and costly programs she did not have the resources to implement.

The budget she submitted in February also made clear her commitment to avoid a progressive income tax. In it she proposed a long list of new taxes and increases in existing taxes. These heft increases which totaled over two hundred million dollars in projected revenues included a request to raise the state's regressive sales tax by one percent to the burdensome level of seven percent. As she had previously announced, the governor did not earmark federal revenue sharing funds for the municipalities. Her budget address, further horrified public and special interest groups with her proposals for major cuts in some human services and for maintenance of last year's funding in others. State workers, too, were shocked by her suggestion that automatic pay increases for civil service employees be eliminated.

True to her promise of open government, Ella held a series of public hearings after she submitted her first budget. Many "underfunded" and "overheated" individuals took full advantage of the opportunity to berate the governor for her broken campaign promises and for her lack of compassion. Those in education and advocates for the handicapped and the mentally retarded lamented the loss of a leader who had been their conduit to the General Assembly during the Ribicoff and Dempsey administrations. State workers also reacted angrily when they learned that their paychecks would be leaner, not fatter, as she had promised during her campaign.

Others pointed out her hypocrisy on the subject of the state income tax. At an energy conference she attended earlier that year, Ella argued that the burden of President Ford's proposed tax on imported oil would fall most heavily on those least able to pay. Ten days later, she promised she would make the burden of her new taxes as "easy as possible" and pledged to spread the levies as "broadly and equitably" as possible. Yet the increased sales tax which would go into effect in April certainly did not spread the burden broadly or equitably; the poor would still bear the brunt of this regressive tax.

Ella faced the intense public criticism alone. Her mentor and closest advisor lay deathly ill in the hospital. Though she continued to consult with Bailey on major appointments, the governor could not and would not involve him in the day-to-day operation of the state. On April 10, four days after she had sent two candidates for state police commissioner to be interviewed by the Chairman, Governor Grasso announced Bailey's death at a crowded press conference. While John Dempsey, Bob Killian, Gloria Schaffer, and other Democrats struggled to keep back the tears and steady their voices, only Ella remained composed. At that moment, the press and the politicians looked to the Party's matriarch. Ella took sole command. Staring straight ahead, with dry eyes, and in a strong voice, she delivered the first eulogy.

The protest to the governor's program did not subside—opposition to Ella's new tax schedule and spending plan culminated almost a month after Bailey's death. On May 7, several hundred state workers, educators, and people in anti-poverty programs descended on the Capitol to voice their protest. They stationed themselves outside the Hall of the House shouting: "Defeat the budget! Defeat the budget!" completely drowning out the floor debate. Welfare lobbyists surrounded the entrance to the governor's office chanting: "We want Ella! Where's Ella?" The ugly scene reminded many of a day a few years before when welfare mothers stormed up to the steps of the Capitol demanding to know where "Tough Tommy" was hiding.

During the tumultuous legislative session, no one missed John Bailey more than Ella Grasso. Not only did she face increasingly unhappy constituencies but she also confronted an undisciplined General Assembly. Even though the Democrats outnumbered the Republicans by 118 to 33 in the House and 29 to 2 in the Senate, the governor's captains in the Legislature could not easily put together a majority to pass her budget. The legislators, many of whom had been elected to their first term in the wave of opposition to Watergate, were leery of Party orders and were unwilling to slash programs that served their constituents. The freshmen lawmakers' refusals to follow Party orders angered Ella, a product of the school of strict Democratic discipline. Her response to their lack of cooperation was a studied aloofness. After much huffing and puffing, however, the Legislators adopted a tax and spending plan close to the one the governor had brought before them a few months before.

The end of the legislative session did not end Ella's troubles. A devout Catholic who opposed abortion on what she said were moral not religious grounds, Ella enraged feminists by endorsing the Social Services Department's decision not to pay for welfare recipients' abortions. Feminists, many of whom had criticized the governor for naming only two women to head major state departments, protested her position. Ella's friend and colleague from her days in Congress, Bella Abzug, chided Ella for her "outrageous" stand on the issue, chastising the governor for "imposing her own beliefs on the public."

Weary of the constant public criticism and from the long hours she had worked in the first nine months of her term, Ella decided to take a vacation with her husband at the end of September. Convinced by close friends and family to travel to Italy, the couple planned to visit the towns in the northern part of the country where their parents had been born. After little more than a week, Ella Grasso cut the trip short because she learned from Nancy Lewinsohn, her chief aide, that heavy rainstorms threatened to cause severe flooding. Anxious to avoid Meskill's fatal mistake of being away from Connecticut during a crisis, Ella rushed home to survey the damage in the state. Though severe flooding never occurred, Mrs. Grasso made it clear to people in the state that their governor was at the Capitol ready to take strong action if necessary. She would not be enjoying a pleasant holiday while her people braved hardships.

Talk of the 1976 Democratic presidential primaries that fall also helped to improve the governor's image. Rule changes for the selection of state delegates to the national convention ordered by the Democratic National Committee led to frequent mention of the potential presidential candidacy of Mrs. Grasso. New procedures for delegate selection called for a primary in all 169 towns. Any candidate that received at least fifteen percent of the Democratic votes would be entitled to national delegates. The Democratic Party organization, which could no longer choose its state delegates at a convention, did get some leeway in that they were granted a category of "uncommitted" delegates. That meant the party organization's leaders could support an uncommitted slate of delegates against the well-known presidential aspirants. Given this wide-open system based on proportional representation and the fact that many in the Connecticut organization were not ready to support any of the already announced candidates—Mo Udall, Scoop Jackson, and Jimmy Carter—the possibility of getting Mrs. Grasso into the political contest began to be widely discussed.

Her candidacy would offer many benefits to the state Party. It would rally the organization behind a single candidate, "a woman who could become the first serious contender for a presidential nomination." It would focus national attention on Connecticut during the peak of state presidential primaries. It would also give the state leaders increased bargaining power and authority at the national convention.

Outside Connecticut, Ella received some support for the 1976 race. Late in September, a committee of New York Democrats announced their efforts to draft her for the Vice Presidential nomination. The group led by Arthur J. Paone, "an average Brooklyn Democrat," hoped to enter a slate of delegates committed to Mrs. Grasso in several New York Congressional districts.

Though frequently mentioned as a "favorite daughter" during that fall, Ella remained publicly removed, as was her custom, from the presidential scurry in the state. She did not permit her name to be put forward in Connecticut as a candidate for the vice presidential or presidential nomination. Although aware of her national stature as the only female governor, Mrs. Grasso knew she would have difficulty drawing a substantial following in her home state especially after the passage of her first budget which had alienated large segments of her strong supporters. She appeared to be having difficulty in distinguishing her austerity administration from that of her predecessor, Thomas Meskill. As one journalist noted, she had introduced little progressive legislation to prove her "presidential timber." The governor, plagued by fiscal problems, apparently did not want to risk a statewide test of her popularity by entering the primary race.

The state's financial situation did not promise her greater popularity. Fiscal year 1975 ended with a deficit of over seventy million dollars. Ella's advisors predicted that even with the additional taxes adopted by the General assembly that year, the state would be approximately eighty million dollars in debt by the close of fiscal 1976. Bent on balancing the books, the governor called the Legislature into special session in an attempt to put Connecticut in the black.

The revenue raising plan Governor Grasso put before the General Assembly in December probably represented one of the worst political mistakes of her quarter century career. Her program attacked two of the most powerful and organized groups in the state—civil servants and veterans. It included a proposal to increase the work week for state employees from thirty-five to forty hours per week without a pay increase and a provision to transfer thirty million dollars from the Soldiers, Sailors, and Marines fund to augment the General Fund. Both of these points in her budget-balancing plan created an uproar among constituents and created a stalemate in the General Assembly. State legislators, stymied by the strong veterans' and state employees' lobbies, adjourned without action on the governor's program. The law-makers' refusal to pass the gubernatorial program or to come up with an alternative solution to the budget crisis caused Mrs. Grasso's popularity to plunge further. Forced to follow through with her threat to tempo-rarily lay off state workers, she fired five hundred employees a few days before Christmas. This edict enraged state employees and their fam-ilies, angered labor groups and provoked heavy criticism in the press.

Ella's proposals and the alternatives she finally chose at the end of the session stood in clear opposition to Bailey politics for they easily alienated two large segments of the electorate. Bailey probably would have advised his pupil to bet on the deficit being reduced by other measures, while keeping her good standing with the civil service employees.

Mrs. Grasso's action relating to the special session did not reflect a wholesale abandonment of the Chairman's principles. Rather, it merely reflected an instance, like the fight for the peace plank at the 1968 convention, when she felt she could risk her political property to gain greater political capital. She no doubt believed that the image of the lazy state worker and the general desire for austerity would rally the public behind her proposal to increase the work week. Yet unlike her brash demand for an end to the Vietnam war, her call for balancing the budget on the backs of veterans and state employees, liquidated large amounts of the political capital she had worked hard to accumulate.

By the end of her first year in office, Governor Grasso had gathered some new political property. The state's unsound fiscal footing had not hampered reform because reform did not cost much money. She moved to restore confidence in government with her landmark freedom of information legislation which she had long championed. It won unanimous support in both houses. New public utilities control authority legislation, though not as strong as she had promised, would provide an independent consumer council with a full-time commissioner who had expertise to guard against automatic fuel adjustment charges. She could demonstrate her commitment to bettering the condition of elderly citizens by pointing to the creation of the new professional Department on Aging. These victories, however, did not balance favorably with the losses.

By the end of her first year in office, Governor Grasso had fulfilled few of her campaign promises; the rest were clearly broken or remained unaddressed. She had not provided corporate tax incentives which would improve employment prospects in the state. She had not provided aid to transportation and her commitment to education had fallen by the wayside in the wake of the budget crisis. Most of these losses indeed, could be attributed to Connecticut's bare cupboard. She could not build programs on a financially unsound foundation.

Still, the people of the state remained disturbed and disappointed that Ella Grasso had gone back on her commitment to provide efficient, compassionate and humane government. Laying off hundreds of workers did not save a significant amount—someone forgot to remember that worker's compensation would necessarily be doled out to those fired from their jobs. Firing five hundred workers saved the state only about five hundred thousand dollars. This drastic measure hardly seemed "efficient." Firing five hundred workers before Christmas was not "compassionate" either. Eliminating paying for abortions for women on welfare was not "humane."

Ella's popularity plunged not merely because she did not make good on her campaign promises as a consequence of the state's fiscal condition. It also plunged because labor, women, and minorities began to realize that their champion was not as "liberal" as they had believed her to be. As governor of a troubled state, she could no longer conceal her stands on issues as she had been able to do in Congress, nor could she rally only behind popular causes as she had the opportunity to do as Secretary of State. As governor in a state with a large debt, she had to make hard decisions and demand unpopular solutions—solutions which sometimes alienated her strongest supporters. As chief executive in Connecticut, she could no longer concentrate all her energies on amassing political capital. She struggled to maintain the property she had once earlier held so easily.

Chapter Nine

CREAM PUFFS AND MERINGUE
1977-1978

When Ella began her second year in office, most legislators foresaw little prospect for improvement of her "tarnished image." In her budget message that opened the regular session, Mrs. Grasso chided the General Assembly for its inaction during the special session and blamed it for the remaining projected thirty million dollar deficit. She prescribed the same unpalatable medicine—an increase in the work week for state employees from thirty-five to forty hours without a commensurate increase in pay and a transfer of twenty-nine million dollars from the Soldiers, Sailors and Marines Fund to the General Fund. To coax her uncooperative "children," she added a proposal for an across-the-board salary increase of three hundred dollars for all state employees and a promise to provide two and one-half million dollars a year to the Veterans' Fund.

Legislators, left with a bad taste in their mouths after the uproar of the state employees during the special session, refused to swallow the governor's civil service cure-all. The enmity of the state workers, who formed a powerful block in the electorate, had not diminished. General Assembly members resoundingly defeated the forty hour week. The Legislature also stood its ground on the veterans issue. It remained reluctant to be accused of "robbing the veterans' piggy bank" begun after World War I when legislators had voted to set aside two cents on every pack of cigarettes to take care of servicemen in times of need. Some legislators, ever mindful of the clout they believed veterans carried among the electorate, opposed the plan to liquidate the Fund because it was politically prudent to "hate what the veterans hate." Others opposed the idea because they were unsure of the amount of the deficit—many considered Mrs. Grasso's fiscal advisors to be extremely conservative and cautious.

Financial observers also displayed skepticism over the governor's fiscal strategies. Moody's Investors Service displayed reluctance to raise the state's financial standing. Although Moody's interests were not with the deficit, it had knocked Connecticut's credit rating down a crucial notch from AA to A1 in response to unsound bonding practices begun in the previous administrations. The firm expressed its concern over what they called "sleazy tactics" in the new budget, namely the "borrowing from or postponing of payments" into the pension fund.

Another major part of Governor Grasso's revenue plan, though it passed in the end, was criticized as harshly as her proposals regarding the state workers and veterans. Republicans and Democrats alike chastized Ella's call to adopt "accrual accounting." The one-time budgetary change she suggested amounted to using twelve months' worth of revenue to finance thirteen months of expenditures. State auditors, non-partisan critics, labeled the scheme "merely an alternative to taxes" or what liberals viewed as a refusal to deal with the question of the personal income tax. Mrs. Grasso's accrual accounting received harsh treatment in the press. Hartford's *Advocate*, prone to printing the most critical commentary on state politics, called the fiscal trick a "mirror" maneuver which allowed her to deflect fiscal responsibility and gain the illusion of solvency. Even *Connecticut Magazine*, relatively more conservative in its orientation, branded Ella's revenue plan "a budget of cream puffs and meringue—plenty of fluff, little substance, and extremely high in fat."

Her budget did lack a substantive program for maintaining solvent state finances during her administration. It contained a collection of remedies to treat only the symptoms rather than the real causes of the state's dwindling revenue base. Ella did not attempt to reallocate state spending into areas where it would be the most productive nor did she try to reform the antiquated tax system. Ella fully intended that Connecticut should continue to rely for the bulk of its revenues on the regressive sales tax.

Governor Grasso chose to oppose the personal income tax for pragmatic political reasons. Chester Bowles lost his re-election bid after strongly advocating the progressive tax during his first term as governor. Abe Ribicoff, on the other hand, had denounced the tax and won two terms. Ella, always aware of prevailing political currents, knew public opinion had changed little since Ribicoff's re-election in 1958. Popular fury against the tax had probably even increased during the 1960s and 1970s; most state politicians of both parties maintained a vigorous stand against the tax.

General Assembly members, many of whom criticized the "gimmicks" Ella used to balance the budget, took the same pragmatic approach to the personal income tax issue. They publicly opposed the governor's stop-gap measures, but would not openly advocate an income tax as a solution to the state's revenue problems. To do so they believed would be certain political suicide. Few had forgotten that in 1971, when the Legislature accidentally passed a personal income tax in an omnibus package in the last moments of the session, Connecticut constituents had been deeply angered. After the 'mistake' was discovered, the General Assembly held a special session just a few weeks later to repeal it. Yet legislators had little to offer as alternatives. Republicans and Democrats refused to request increases in other existing taxes to scrape up funds. At seven percent, the sales tax was the highest in the nation. Burdensome taxes on business were already driving businesses and industries out of the state at an alarming rate. Because the Legislature did not want to institute an income tax or increase existing taxes they were left with little choice but to ratify accrual accounting and similar strategies. The Legislature's refusal to deal directly with the state's revenue problems and acceptance of Grasso's gimmicks earned it the title of the "House of Mirrors."

A few liberal legislators did openly support an income tax. Irving Stolberg, a House Democrat from New Haven, became one of the most vocal advocates of the tax, while Audrey Beck, a Democrat from

Storrs, led the forces in the Senate. James Kennelly, a Hartford politician who had married John Bailey's daughter, Barbara, also made pitches for a personal income tax, including a plea for serious consideration of the unpopular levy in a page-long editorial in *Connecticut Magazine*. Still, Stolberg, Beck, and Kennelly drew only a few followers. Mostly they received sharp criticism from their colleagues. Governor Grasso reacted particularly strongly against Beck's efforts to stir up sentiment for a state tax on personal income.

As the leader of the Senate finance committee, Beck had incurred the governor's wrath by blocking many of her budget proposals. In a fit of rage over her general lack of cooperation and what she considered the senator's impertinence, Ella lashed out at Beck, accusing her of "lusting after" an income tax— a crime Connecticut citizens considered only somewhat less heinous than treason and murder.

Despite the many difficulties, Governor Grasso proved ready to stay the storm over her budget of "gimmicks," a budget held together with "Scotch tape and prayers." In order to keep the campaign promise she cared about most—state solvency without an income tax—Ella continually threatened legislators that a large deficit would accumulate if they did not agree to accrual accounting and her other austerity measures. She consistently lamented the size of the projected deficit, rarely disclosing the amount of the actual state debt. She remained willing to sacrifice her popularity early in her administration in hopes she would sweep a surplus large enough to avoid serious consideration of an income tax during her first term.

With her budget proposals under constant criticism and without Bailey to command the 'troops' in the General Assembly, Ella's political problems continued. She could not pass her League of Women Voters-style reform program. Her captains in the Democratic House and Senate, many of them miffed because she had consulted them only infrequently, did not deliver a stronger state gambling commission, a reorganized Special Revenue Commission, higher education structure, a new set of more open primary laws, nor a bottle bill. After her many failures in the Legislature, Ella cut off communication with her Party's majority leadership, withdrawing into the quiet recesses of her office, watched over by her "palace guard." The loss of her closest advisor,

John Bailey, and of her strong supporters in the state's biggest cities—
Nick Carbone of Hartford and Arthur Barbieri of New Haven—
through personal conflicts, led her to a lonely political existence during
her second year in office.

The governor's political woes worsened when she chose wrongly in
the contest for the Democratic presidential nomination for 1976. Eager
to be identified with a front-running, successful candidate, Ella came
out for the early leader, Henry "Scoop" Jackson, with whom she had
been acquainted and whose moderate positions she had shared in her
Congressional days. While other Connecticut Democrats declared
their neutrality in a race difficult to call, Ella started stumping for the
middle-of-the-road senator from Washington state. At several campaign stops, Jackson alluded to the possibility that he would choose Ella
as his Vice Presidential running mate. In the spring, his candidacy, like
Muskie's four years before, began to fizzle. Still Grasso stayed staunchly
behind "Scoop" to keep her dignity among state Democrats. To her
embarrassment, Jackson fell far behind Carter and Udall in Connecticut's May primary. Carbone, her "foremost antagonist" in the party
and a leader of the state's Carter organization, exulted in Ella's incor-
rect choice.

To regain her political momentum, Grasso needed to select a shrewd
advisor and a skilled strategist. Ella decided that Bill O'Neill, successor
to John Bailey as State Chairman and House majority leader, could not
fulfill these roles. He hadn't delivered the Democratic vote behind her
budget and reform programs. They had disagreed over candidates for
the Presidential nomination. In the heat of that uncomfortable political summer, Ella asked O'Neill to give up the Chairmanship, arguing
that no person could head both the party and the Legislature. He
refused to step down. In August, she moved to unseat him, but O'Neill
easily defeated her choice, Peter Kelly of Hartford.

Ella knew when she was licked. Knowing she had no other alternative but to follow Bailey's favorite axiom "If you can't beat 'em, join
'em," the governor participated in truce talks arranged by John Dempsey, Sr. to resolve her differences with O'Neill. Ella opened relatively
friendly lines of communication with the Party Chairman and House
majority leader for her fortunes would depend heavily on his favor.

Bailey had trained her well enough to know she needed his support during the next legislative session. She did not, however, forgive and forget as the Boss had done many times in his long political career. Ella, whose vindictiveness impelled her to keep a clear mental record of every colleague who crossed her on the smallest of issues, refused to forget that O'Neill opposed her or to forgive him for causing her political trouble. She would get even later.

To save her political skin, Ella also came out quickly in support of Jimmy Carter. On June 12, the peanut farmer and former governor of Georgia called to ask for her support, ending the coolness that had existed between the two. On June 13, the governor of Connecticut held a press conference to announce that she would be campaigning for Mr. Carter. She traveled in the midwest to deliver speeches backing him for President as well as to enhance her own national reputation. In mid-July Ella again won recognition throughout the country when she co-chaired the party's national convention. After the November election, rumors flew that the new Democratic administration would permanently bail Ella out of her continuing political problems by granting her a position as Ambassador to Italy or as a member of the Carter cabinet. But the governor had already announced her intention to seek re-election. The Windsor Locks native wanted to stay in the state.

To escape her political troubles and renew her physical strength, Ella retreated to her large, but modest home in Old Lyme, which she and Tom had bought during her first term as governor. On Friday afternoons, she left the crowded Capitol city and began the familiar journey to the shore along with thousands of other Connecticut commuters. The hour-long drive brought her to a quiet dead-end street not far from the center of town, the beach, and an exclusive country club.

Ella would usually dine at a nearby restaurant with a few friends on Friday evening. On Saturday she would rise early and walk over to the Old Lyme Public Library where she would spend several hours reading popular magazines that she refused to subscribe to because she thought them too expensive. After stopping at the library, she liked to visit Scott's orchards or another of the fruit and vegetable stands in the area.

She admired the merchandise and chatted easily with the shoppers, many of whom did not recognize her as their governor.

Ella enjoyed her relative anonymity on the weekends and would often drive over to the neighboring town of Essex, where even fewer people seemed to recognize her. During her frequent visits to the town, she made a few friends among the proprietors of the small business establishments and restaurants on the Main Street. She liked to browse in the curio shops and then have luncheon with a friend at the Griswold Inn. In the afternoons she would wander about the town alone or she would return to Old Lyme and take a long walk with her husband Tom.

Ella spent spring and summer Saturdays working in her garden at the shore. Though the wildflowers she tried to transplant never lived more than a few days in the sandy soil, several plants survived and even thrived in Ella's rather scraggly garden. A yellow rose bush brought as a gift from Texas by Lyndon Johnson bore many blossoms. Ella always kept a bright band of marigolds bordering the backyard; and she always managed to raise a bumper crop of cherry tomatoes that would have made papa Tambussi proud.

When Ella planted the first seedlings in her garden in the spring, she also began to plan for her favorite holiday—Christmas. She loved buying, making, wrapping, and giving presents; everyone of her friends received a gift which she or her state trooper would deliver. It was rare for her to enter a store and emerge empty handed, for she was inevitably reminded of a particular friend or relative as she scanned the shelves and displays. She worked on needlepoint pillows and presented them her special personal and political friends. Often she took considerable time and trouble to create or select an appropriate gift. When she decided to stitch a pillow for her close political advisor, Chad Mc-Collam, who owned a cottage on Block Island, she called up the efforts of the State Department of Environmental Protection and got a definitive map of the island transferred to needlepoint canvas. When she learned on of her female friends was interested in Egyptology, she sought out a renowned archeologist to autograph a catalogue of the Tutankamen exhibit.

All of Ella's closets at the governor's residence and in her homes in

Windsor Locks and in Old Lyme were filled with Christmas presents that she wrapped herself. Her husband, children and staff at the residence had grown accustomed to finding her sitting on the floor surrounded by rolls of wrapping and tissue papers, ribbons and bows. After several hours of struggling with a few feet of paper and several yards of tape, she would stand up and proudly display a small pile of wrapped presents that would be stowed away with scores of others until they would be delivered.

Susanne frequently accompanied her mother on many of Ella's Christmas shopping tours. She often met her mother after work on Friday afternoons and the two would drive down to Old Lyme together where they would spend a quiet weekend shopping, cooking and talking like college roommates. Both women shared a love of Italian culture, art, and literature.

A talented visual artist, Susanne chose to follow a different career path than her mother. She attended Loomis Chafe almost three decades after her mother was a day student there. Then she enrolled in the prestigious art school, The Rhode Island School of Design. She continued her studies at the Trinity College in Dublin and at the Jagelonia University in Cracow and returned to Connecticut to teach art at the University of Hartford. She later joined the commercial art department of the Hartford Insurance Group where the famed poet Wallace Stephens had earned his livelihood.

Jimmy, three years Susanne's junior, also returned to Connecticut after finishing his undergraduate studies. His interest in the armed forces led him to take a job with the Adjutant General in Hartford. Ella, who liked to keep a watchful eye on her children, was undoubtedly pleased that both her children were close by. Jimmy's office at the Armory was directly adjacent to the Capitol and Susanne's office was only a few blocks from Hartford's Bushnell Park. Highly interested in her children's daily activities, Ella kept in close contact with Susanne and Jimmy. Rarely a day passed without some word from Mother Ella. Even when the normal means of communication were unavailable, Ella managed to get word to her children. When Susane was studying in England and staying in a hotel room without a telephone, Ella got calls through to her daughter on the landlord's telephone. Another time when Susanne was studying at the Jagelonia University, Ella managed to get a message through to her daughter, despite the slow mails and strict security in Cracow. At Jagelonia University just over a week, Susanne, who was staying in a dorm with over 1500 students, was greeted by an unfamiliar middle-aged man in the lobby. Giving his name, the man said he was from New Britain, Connecticut. He handed her a note written by Ella and asked her to call her mother immediately. Susanne, who could not place a telephone call from the dorm sent off a telegram to her mother before she went to her next class.

By the end of the year, Ella had less reason to consider leaving Connecticut for a more secure national administrative post. Fiscal year 1976 showed a surplus of thirty-five million dollars instead of the eighty million dollar deficit she had predicted. The surplus was brought about by accrual accounting as well as a one cent per gallon increase in the state gasoline tax she had managed to convince the Legislature to pass. A substantial part of the excess could also be attributed to a new lottery which Ella, an avid opponent of gaming, had allowed to pass in the General Assembly. The governor remained silent on the money-making lottery because when the Legislature did not pass her proposed two cent per gallon gas tax, she was left without a substantial amount of expected revenue. So the pragmatic Mrs. Grasso accepted the profitable new numbers game, despite her strong personal distaste for it.

Once she achieved a fiscal surplus, Ella began to pick up the pieces of her shattered political image. In the state address she delivered in January of 1977, Governor Grasso targeted some of her new resources to areas in which she had lost heavy support. She pledged to rehire all of the state workers she had fired and promised to increase the wages of civil service employees. More dollars in the state till meant she could finally fulfill many of her campaign promises by giving greater funding to the departments she helped create and the programs she favored. She called for substantial increases in the budgets of the departments of Consumer Protection and Aging. She spoke of the necessity for increased funding for the Freedom of Information Commisson. She proposed a one and one-half million dollar job training program tailored to meet both the needs of the urban unemployed and the state's new industries. A final aspect of her program proved particularly appealing—she did not recommend any new or higher taxes.

Simultaneously, Governor Grasso began a new effort aimed at strengthening her relationship with the General Assembly to ensure passage of her legislative program. Ella kept up cordial communication with House Majority leader O'Neill. She made it clear to Senate majority leader Joseph Lieberman, former follower and biographer of John Bailey, that she needed his cooperation. The "warm personal friendship" which grew between President Pro Tempore of the Senate, Joseph Fauliso and the governor, also helped this endeavor.

By the beginning of 1977, Ella had also begun to make friends with business. In her first term, she had stressed economic development because economic growth would mean more jobs for "her people." Working with her likeable and extremely capable Commissioner of Economic Development, Edward Stockton, the governor launched an ambitious campaign to improve the state's business climate. They vigorously promoted legislation providing tax incentives for industries to locate or expand in Connecticut. Stockton held a number of successful conferences that gave prospective investors a chance to meet the governor as well as other state business leaders. The commissioner and the governor made several trips to Europe to talk with interested foreign business people considering coming to the United States. These efforts effectively reversed the trend of firms leaving the state to locate in the sunbelt. Large enterprises such as Union Carbide, Boehringer Ingleheim, General Dynamics, Eastern Data Service, American Airlines, and General Host joined the Connecticut business community. Ella's economic development project proved to be one of the most productive programs during her first term and seemed to give her confidence and satisfaction. She took pleasure in "turning the traditional shovel of earth to break ground for a new factory."

Ella's activism in improving the state's business climate brought her closer to leaders in the private sector whose expertise she tapped for her reform and reorganization programs. Ella enlisted the energies of Clayton Gengras, extremely successful in business and her new neighbor on Prospect Avenue. She convinced Gengras, both a millionaire and a former Republican gubernatorial candidate, to head the "Committee on the Structure of State Government" created to improve the state's management efficiency. John Filer, President of Aetna Life and Casualty (one of the largest insurance companies in Hartford, the nation's insurance capitol), agreed to chair the governor's other major "blue ribbon" committee on government reorganization. Filer's "Commission for Better Government through Reorganization" was charged with submitting proposals to streamline government structures.

When the Legislature convened for the 1977 session, it accepted most of the Filer Commission's plan that reorganized more than two hundred state offices into twenty-two departments. Passage of the reorganization legislation pleased the governor; it attested not only to the improvement of her relationship with the General assembly but also to the strength of her partnership with business.

Unwilling to lose the favor of the business community, Ella chose to abandon her old friendship with organized labor by ultimately supporting a bill backed by the Connecticut Business and Industry Association, the top lobbyist for state business. The CBIA's bill, dubbed "quits and fires", denied unemployed compensation to workers who quit their jobs or who were fired for misconduct. Ella disliked the dilemma "quits and fires" posed: if she supported it, labor would be against her; if she rejected it business would be against her. Labor's refusal, however, to forgive her for firing the five hundred state employees no doubt led her to side with management. And with the 1978 elections fast approaching, she probably felt she could not afford to lose one of the few friendly forces in her first team performance—a cooperative business community. Hartford City Councilman Carbone, an increasingly vocal critic of the governor and of the moderate wing of the Democratic party, attacked Ella for her anti-labor stance and later accused her of "turning over the reigns of government" to a Republican, E. Clayton Gengras.

The governor's budget also provided the "street-fighting" councilman with more fuel for his claim that Ella was ignoring the urban poor. Mrs. Grasso had proposed only a five percent increase in benefits for welfare recipients. Carbone called for a twenty percent increase in benefits which would bring the payments up from the 1971 level to the 1974 level. When Ella refused to budge, arguing for austerity, he launched a crusade for more money for welfare recipients, urban centers, and bi-lingual education programs. He traveled around the state calling Grasso and her followers "cheapos" and attempted to form a new political coalition to successfully pressure the General Assembly for more money for the cities. Carbone's efforts, combined with those of Lieberman, Kennelly and other Democratic leaders from large cities forced a ten percent hike in benefits as well as several million dollars of additional aid in the form of rent assistance for recipients.

Incensed over the welfare and other spending increases that brought the budget forty million dollars over what she had recommended, Ella responded with what a *Courant* writer called "political gimmickry." Governor Grasso scolded the general Assembly for its lack of thrift and announced she would not sign the budget until cuts were made. Ella did not, however, offer suggestions for where cuts could be made nor did she give reasons for her action. She further enraged legislators by leaving the state to attend a conference while they struggled over the budget package. The lawmakers, tired after the tough session and weary of lack of leadership in setting priorities for slashing spending, refused to change the budget. Determined not to shoulder the responsibility of a deficit if it occurred in the next fiscal year because of unexpected increases, Ella refused to sign the budget.

Three months after the 1978 budget became law without her signature, fiscal year 1977 ended with a one hundred and nine million dollar surplus. Ella's spending restraints aided by a resurgence in the state's economic health created the second consecutive surplus. Ella's strategies, though they successfully produced the economic outcomes she planned, did not secure the political effects she had anticipated. Her achievement of a balanced budget through austerity had not enhanced her popularity in the statehouse or among her Connecticut constituents. Rather, the opposite occurred. By the end of 1977, political events of the summer and fall had cast considerable doubt upon her candidacy for the next year's gubernatorial election.

In mid-June, Nicholas Carbone registered his opposition to Ella Grasso's candidacy in the 1978 race on the weekly Connecticut current affairs television program "Face the State". He also called for a state-wide primary which would elimiante a state convention and open up the process for selecting Democratic candidates. A few days later, a poll taken by New Haven Democratic leaders showed a "negative reaction" to Ella Grasso's first administration—16% of those surveyed rated her performance "poor", 40% felt she had done a "fair" job, 30% said she had done a "good" job, and only 7% gave her "excellent" marks. The same day the New Haven leaders released the poor results to the press, the Caucus of Connecticut Democrats, founded by the liberal peace activists Joe Duffy and Ann Wexler, announced their resolve to "support a progressive candidate." Governor Grasso would not be the candidate they sought to nominate. While the CCD, chaired by Mary Sullivan, started its search for a candidate to the left of Mrs. Grasso, Nick Carbone launched a state-wide campaign to unseat her. In September, Boss Barbieri of New Haven joined Carbone's forces because he was allegedly disgruntled over Grasso's decision not to appoint him as liquor commissioner.

In an attempt to squelch the opposition, whose major charge against the governor lay in her lack of attention to urban issues, Ella held a press conference to announce the creation of a cabinet-level team of state officials "to speed and coordinate" federal and state aid programs to help Connecticut's under-funded cities. This action probably had little influence on her popularity as reflected in the polls.

A major poll commissioned by Joe Lieberman, a New Haven Democrat, gave Grasso a favorable rating of 37%. Congress members Chris Dodd and Toby Moffett respectively led the list of favored Democrats for the gubernatorial nomination. Neither one, however, wanted to enter the race. Predictably a poll taken by the Connecticut State Employees' Association revealed that the governor received only 5% of the vote for the 1978 election. Also predictable was a poll taken in conservative Fairfield county which gave Grasso a 61% favorable rating.

Seemingly undaunted by the polls, Ella announced her intention to seek reelection on November 29, ending speculation about her interest in taking over the Presidency of Mount Holyoke College or Yale University.

Encouraged by the slump in the polls Robert Killian decided to challenge Mrs. Grasso for the Democratic nomination for the office he long coveted. Carbone and other disaffected Democratic liberals strengthened Killian's cause by rallying behind the lieutenant governor's candidacy. Poll results and the general perception that Ella's support had been significantly lessened led Republican congress member Ronald Sarasin to consider risking his Washington seat for the highest office at the statehouse. By the end of 1977, Bob Killian and Ron Sarasin felt confident enough about their political fortunes that they both had announced their intention to run for governor. Ella's challengers believed that the governor had already sealed her fate with her inept handling of the budget and urban affairs issues. After major blunders in these areas, repair of her badly damaged reputation appeared highly unlikely.

For the first time in twenty years, Ella's chances for election to public office looked bleak. Not only did the polls look unfavorable, but her party was dividing against her. The liberal opposition led by Nick Carbone was getting strong media attention. Her own lieutenant governor was running against her, an unthinkable move by Bailey standards. The strength of support she could receive from women, labor, big city leaders, and educators was certainly in doubt. Despite these major problems, Ella stuck by her decision to seek re-election. She was afraid of losing an election—she had never lost one during her long career. Yet she appeared more terrified of being without a job in public office. At age 59, she did not want to retire. She did not want to, and probably could not, run for Congress again. Nor did she want a position in the Carter administration, because she did not want to go to Washington. Mrs. Grasso wanted to stay in Connecticut and she wanted to be governor.

Chapter Ten

MOTHER ELLA
1978

*"You don't always like what your
mother does, but she's still your mother."*

Michael Riley on Ella Grasso.

Ella Grasso's popularity had reached its lowest point when a severe blizzard struck the state in the first weeks of February, 1978. Across Connecticut, the storm dumped eighteen inches of snow while fifty mile-per-hour winds piled drifts of over fifteen feet. For the first time in forty years, postal carriers could not deliver mail. Bradley International Airport shut down for a day. Schools all over the state remained closed for a week.

The heavy snow began to fall early on February 7. By mid-day, most employers had dismissed their workers and schools had stopped classes. Driving conditions worsened as everyone tried to get home. As Ella returned to her office after a morning of speeches, her chauffeured state police car got stuck in a traffic jam on Farmington Avenue. Impatient and anxious to get back to the Capitol so that she could direct snow removal operations, the governor left her driver and began to make her way toward Capitol Avenue on foot. Trudging through the snow, already about six inches deep, she encountered motorists stopped in their cars along the major downtown arteries, and they beeped their horns and waved as she passed them on her mile-long trek.

When the governor reached her office, staff members briefed her on the severity of the storm. Then she walked over to the Armory next door to the Capitol, where she set up headquarters, and took charge of emergency operations. Soon after she arrived at the Armory, Ella issued a directive closing all state highways so that roads could be cleared. This order effectively halted the activities of Connecticut's businesses and industries. She issued orders for supplies to various shelters and dispatched extra pieces of heavy equipment for snow removal. She telephoned Washington to ask the President to declare the state a disaster area and ask for federal assistance. She even spent the night at the Armory, catching a few hours of sleep on an office sofa.

During the crisis, Ella did not forget about the political consequences of her actions. The governor wanted her people to know that, unlike her predecessor, Thomas Meskill, she would be with them and at the helm—in command, in control. She allowed reporters free-run of the Armory, held frequent press conferences, and granted many television and radio interviews throughout the evening and the next day. Stranded in their homes with little to do but to watch television and listen to the radio, her constituents saw their matronly, middle-aged governor give live reports on weather conditions. They listened to Ella give words of encouragement in her simple language and maternal voice. When they opened their newspapers, they read about the helicopter tour of the state she made to assess the damage. Her people reached out to her for help. One Norwich man registered a particularly poignant plea to the governor. In an open field, he stamped a huge message in the snow that was visible from an altitude of 2,000 feet: "HELP ELLA!"

Ella's desire to occupy center stage led her to enlist National Guard helicopters so that she and her press entourage could survey the situation first-hand. Before she made stops in the towns hardest hit by the storm, her press group, filling four National Guard helicopters, arrived ahead of her. Some critics said she got carried away with her media theatrics. Her Republican opponent, Ron Sarasin, charged that after promising to stop in an eastern Connecticut town ravaged by the storm, she sent down her press people, who took pictures of her landing, and then left the town without checking the damage or talking to the local officials.

Grasso also took advantage of the opportunity to squelch her Democratic rival, Robert Killian. During the crisis, Grasso refused to assign any tasks to the lieutenant governor. While Ella basked in the limelight, Killian suffered anonymity and humiliation. Mrs. Grasso let Killian, who arrived at the Armory almost a day after she had, pace around aimlessly with nothing to do. Frustrated and impatient, he "ambled" about the suite, "trying his damndest to look important." Mrs. Grasso added further insult: when a reporter asked what Mr. Killian could do to help, she answered: "Oh, is he here? Well, he could make some coffee."

When the storm ended, Ella emerged once again as "Mother Ella" "—compassionate, strong...maternal." Her popularity soared as a result of her superb handling of the crisis and her shrewd manipulation of the media. Once again, the people of Connecticut felt reassured about Ella's caring and concern. Once again, they felt close to the woman they had elected as their governor. Though neither fully recognized the strength of Connecticut's renewed confidence in Mrs. Grasso, both Sarasin and Killian immediately began to feel that their candidacies had been weakened considerably by the storm.

Ella Grasso's "mothering" became a major issue in the campaign. Though at campaign functions she often spoke of her first term accomplishments—solvent state finances, 200,000 jobs, and lower taxes— she preferred to spend most of her time mingling with the crowd rather than discussing her platform. A striking example of this style was her performance at an annual street festival in Hartford's Italian South End. After briefly addressing the crowd "in the round syllables of her parent's native language," she began marching up Franklin Avenue amidst the crowd. Spying a sick old man in a wheelchair, she ran to him, hugged him and kissed his forehead. The crowd made a circle around her, "giving way and falling silent as if in the presence of a healing saint." Neither Killian nor Sarasin could begin to generate the warmth Ella exuded.

Part of Ella's rapport with constituents could be linked to her ethnicity—she understood the concerns and culture of the state's many ethnic Americans, and they, in turn, identified with her. She spoke their language and still lived in the working-class neighborhood of Windsor Locks. She was "everybody's neighbor." Her femininity formed another important dimension of her strong appeal. A reporter who observed her activity at the Franklin Avenue festival noted this essential factor:

> What male candidate, even if he could bring himself to do it, could win votes by embracing the sick?

Mrs. Grasso was aware of the power of her maternal image and made full use of it during the campaign.

Ella consciously cultivated this style, using it effectively in the administration of her day-to-day duties once she was elected governor. A telling example of Ella's maternalism can be found in her handling of constituents opposing mandatory motorcycle helmet legislation. One day when the issue was being debated, many motorcyclists protesting the law descended upon the Capitol, demanding to see the governor. Mrs. Grasso brought the large group, donned in leather jackets and riding boots, into her conference room. The motorcyclists sauntered in and proceeded to register their displeasure in loud voices. Unruffled, Ella used her convincing maternal tone to tame the angry band. "But you're all my children," she argued. "I can't let you go out and hurt yourselves." After that, the motorcyclists filed meekly out of her office and drove quietly away.

Governor Grasso's acting skills made the Mother Ella image believable even when she was feeling less than maternal. One morning Ella held a staff meeting at which she threw a violent tantrum. As one observer described the scene, someone interrupted her yelling and screaming with word that a group of elementary school students were waiting outside to see her. She got up, left her staff, slammed the door behind her, and walked into the outer office to greet them graciously: "Well, H-e-l-l-o-o-o, children. How are you today?" Another time she flew into a rage over campaign signs a few minutes before she was to cut a campaign commercial. She screamed and cursed at her staff and then walked off to tape the television advertisement five minutes later.

Yet, Mrs. Grasso's mothering was genuine. She expressed personal interest and concern for those immediately around her. With her staff, she played matchmaker, commented on their clothing, traded information on bargain stores, and urged them to take care of their health. During long legislative sessions she invited legislators who lived far away from Hartford to stay overnight at the governor's residence. She tried to get Congress member Stewart McKinney to stop smoking. Mrs. Grasso liked to think of herself as a surrogate mother not only for her staff and colleagues, but also for the entire state. A few days after the blizzard, light snow started to fall. Mike Riley, a clerk for the Appropriations Committee, spotted Ella on a floor above. He called up to her: "Governor, it's snowing out. What are you going to do about it?" "Don't worry," she replied, "mother is here, mother is here."

Ella used her mothering perhaps most effectively on the press. She deliberately developed a personal, maternal relationship with the Hartford journalists that precluded hostile or highly critical commentary on her administration. Governor Grasso knew all the reporters by name and referred to members of the Capitol press corps as "my children." One reporter's baby was "our baby." Another young reporter who was consistently tardy to her press conferences, was "my little lost angel." Early in the mornings Ella often wandered into the press room across the hall from her office where writers for state papers and wire services worked. Sometimes she brought Italian pastries to Jim Mutrie, a reporter who wrote for the *New Haven Register* during the Bailey era. She would walk to the back of the press room, seeking out Mutrie and other senior state reporters she knew well. Soon the younger reporters would be in the back of the room listening to Ella and the older reporters exchanging witty remarks. Ella also made it a point to arrive early at her press conferences so that she could engage in lively banter with her press corps. Once the conference began, she worried little about hostile questions; it was difficult for reporters to grill the governor when she had already poured them coffee, inquired about their spouses, or given them a hug five minutes before.

When a reporter did venture to pose a difficult question or ask about an issue she did not wish to talk about, Ella easily avoided it. She didn't try to talk around the issue, she just talked about something else, as one member of the Hartford press corps observed:

> If reporters wanted to know about the budget, Ella Grasso would bring them a little doll which a crippled child had given her, and she'd talk about that. If you wanted to know about taxes, she would tell you about a frog she was entering in a frog-jumping contest. When there were bats in the fifth floor press room and the reporters hinted for an exterminator, she told about the time Tom Grasso killed a bat in the kitchen with a raw potato.

When journalists came to conduct personal interviews with the governor for longer stories, Ella avoided their probing questions by using her favorite conversational ploy—telling homely tales about her childhood. Reporters emerged from private conferences with homespun stories about the Depression in Windsor Locks, her father's bakery, and how she worked to pay for her books at Chaffee.

Ella even managed to get reporters to help her avoid answering tough questions. During a WTIC radio talk show program on which the governor appeared as a guest, a woman called to ask the governor if she was in favor of busing for school desegregation. Mrs. Grasso answered: "We're careful of our kids when they ride school buses." When the woman pressed her, asking the governor again to articulate her stand, Ella replied: "We must be particularly careful of our children in the winter." The woman tried once more to get Mrs. Grasso to commit herself, but the talk show host attacked the listener, telling her the governor had already answered her question. Then the host cut off the woman's call.

Ella ran the press conferences like the proverbial "school teacher." She sat at the crowded press table in Room 212, with her glasses pushed up on her forehead, gazing sternly at the reporters around her. Unlike Meskill, she dominated the discussion and successfully steered the media to topics she cared to comment on. When a journalist interrupted her lesson, wanting to switch to another subject she didn't want to discuss, Mrs. Grasso merely smiled and shook her head. Or she responded to a question she viewed as offensive by saying sharply: "That judgment is yet to be determined." Another reason reporters rarely stepped out of line was that Mrs. Grasso held the press conferences so frequently, even veteran press people had trouble finding "anything new to ask her."

Fear also kept reporters from asking hard questions and printing highly critical stories. Most reporters tried to avoid Mrs. Grasso's vindictiveness, which was well-known in media circles. Gail Collins, a political columnist for the *Hartford Advocate* did not escape the governor's wrath. The *Advocate*, noted for its sharp and often biting liberal critiques of politics, published Collins' pieces which often found fault with Mrs. Grasso and her administration. Even though she had attended many press conferences at the Capitol, Collins had never spoken with the governor. One day the writer was talking to Representative John Groppo; hoping to smooth things over between the two, he said: "Governor, have you met Gail Collins?" Grasso looked Collins straight in the eye, then turned her back and walked away without saying a word. Another time the governor went on an official out-of-state trip accompanied by the usual small group of reporters. These reporters would often depend on her for "the quick travel connections that go with the privilege of power." One journalist in the group had hoped to get a ride back from the meeting with the governor. Aides told him the plane was full so he was forced to spend many hours to get back to Connecticut. Soon after the incident, he found out that Mrs. Grasso's plane had had open seats—the governor merely had "been miffed at one of the reporter's recent stories."

Although Ella may have witheld some information from the press through her tactics of evasion, she was generally more accessible to the press than had been her predecessor. Because her personality and style made her comfortable talking to reporters, she held press conferences more frequently than Thomas Meskill who usually spoke with reporters only a few times a month. And Grasso, unlike Meskill, allowed television cameras and radio microphones at the conferences. Hence, Grasso did take steps to widen the relations between the governor's office and the press during both of her administrations.

Ella sometimes treated her department heads as she did her press corps. Fear of Ella's quick temper and vindictiveness kept her commissioners in line. Her department heads proved timid when talking to the press. Mrs. Grasso, an early riser, read the morning edition of the *Hartford Courant* thoroughly before seven o'clock. If she perceived a comment by one of her commissioners to be directly or indirectly unflattering to her administration, Ella did not hesitate to telephone the executive in question at that early hour and demand an explanation. She also did not hesitate to make early calls to her closest advisors to ask why the "SOB" (referring to the reporter who wrote the offensive article) "wrote that about me."

Incidences of Ella's vindictiveness occurred at several points during the 1978 campaign. One of her opponents remarked after the campaign that Mrs. Grasso could be "brutal, foul-mouthed, and bitchy." The incidents the press reported during the gubernatorial race seem to bear this out. When Killian's candidacy was still in doubt, a reporter asked the governor whether any possibility of a truce existed. Ella answered: "Are there miracles in this century?" At a private party she reportedly called Killian a "son-of-a-bitch." At the Democratic state convention, Robert Killian, Jr. met Ella and her husband in a hallway. The younger Killian greeted Mrs. Grasso: "Hello, governor." Ella told him to "move his ass." Her husband followed up with the suggestion that Killian go "get himself something to eat." Though these incidents revealed a wholly different private self from the pubic image she portrayed, the people of Connecticut remained devoted to the "compassionate, concerned, church-going" Mother Ella.

Ella's actions were often as sharp as her words. One evening, a wealthy stockbroker friend of her daughter's invited Ella and Susanne to join him for what they believed would be an intimate dinner at the elegant Signature restaurant in Hartford. When the two arrived, they saw that nearly a dozen New York business people were already seated, apparently waiting to meet the governor. By the time Ella and Susanne had been seated at opposite ends of the long table, they both silently acknowledged the unexpected situation. After lengthy introductions were made and appetizers were served, Ella looked past all the middle-aged male faces to her daughter. She asked Susanne if her salmon was cooked to her taste. Susanne answered that it was and inquired about her mother's oysters. Dispensing with the usual protocol of posh restaurants, Ella turned to her neighbor and ordered him to pass her appetizer to Susanne. The plate was duly passed by half a dozen pairs of hands. Susanne sensing her mother's motives, passed her own appetizer down for her mother to sample. They continued to exchange their plates throughout the seven course meal, which left little time to discuss whatever business had been on the agenda.

Ella easily steamrollered her two opponents with her shrewd political strategies. Facing an Irish opponent for the party nomination, Ella followed Bailey rules and chose Billy O'Neill, a man of Irish descent, as her campaign manager. She mobilized the many political allies she had acquired across the state during her two decades in Connecticut politics. Killian, whose political base existed mainly in the Hartford area, could not gather great support in other parts of the state. Consequently at the 1978 convention, the first in thirty-two years to choose a state ticket without John Bailey, Ella Grasso almost prevented Killian from gaining the twenty percent needed for an open direct primary.

Though Killian directed his campaign at Ella's weakest points, particularly her record in urban affairs, Ella maintained a strong edge over her challenger. She boasted of her fiscal surpluses and the 200,000 new jobs created during her administration. Those two accomplishments were important to the huge suburban and rural segments that Carbone, Killian's major supporter, had alienated with his strong demands for increased aid to cities. Killian, who lacked Ella's ties to Party leadership, could not turn out the troops. The party's rank and file emerged in full force behind the governor. On September 12, Ella won the only Democratic primary she ever entered. She soundly defeated Killian 137,466, to 66,038, carrying 167 of the state's 169 municipalities.

Ella used the customary tactic of manipulating the budget as a weapon against her Republican challenger, Ron Sarasin. Governor Grasso's 1978 budget showed an increase of eleven percent in the General Fund, which contrasted sharply with the three percent increases she had proposed in non-election years. She dumped the 115 million dollars she had accumulated in surpluses during her first three years into social services. The Departments of Mental Health, Mental Retardation, and Youth Services all got significant funding increases. Ella also targeted additional aid for the poor, the elderly and the unemployed. Every municipality got more state dollars to pay for essential programs to lessen the local property tax. Blighted urban areas received special attention. Hartford got 44.5 million dollars, an increase of about 34% of the previous year's figure; Bridgeport got 33 million dollars, an increase of 45%. State employees got salary increases. Industry got new sources of grants and loans for expansion as well as a reduction in business taxes.

To her list of accomplishments, namely, three surpluses and 200,000 jobs, Ella added the somewhat inaccurate claim of "no new taxes." True she had reduced the tax on business services from 7 to 3.5 percent, but this tax did not exist until she took office. She raised the capital gains tax from 6 to 7 percent and the tax on corporate profits from 8 to 10 percent. She imposed a new tax on dividends and increased the state gasoline tax by 1 cent per gallon. During her administration, in fact, approximately one billion dollars in new taxes had been added. Mrs. Grasso did not, as her claim led many to believe, manage to accumulate a surplus and cut taxes at the same time.

The passage of her most attractive budget package and her exploitation of its political advantages helped her to regain support in areas where she had lost it, once again making her all things to all people. Ella had the Appropriations Committee make detailed lists of how much state money had been funneled to each municipality during her administration. These lists became her campaign bible. She took them with her to every city and town that she visited and told her people what she had done for them.

Ella also won back support from feminists despite her unpopular stands on women's issues. Betty Hudson (who had introduced the legislation to provide state funding for abortions for women on welfare that Ella vetoed) and Audrey Beck issued an appeal to feminists across the state to work for the governor's re-election. They were willing to forget some of Ella's actions which they believed were against women to support the larger cause of women in politics. They were aware of Ella Grasso's power and wanted to rally behind her. "We're supportive of her as a female governor, as the best representative of women in the state," they said. "No governor is going to have a perfect list of what we want."

Despite her inaccuracy on the tax issue and the criticism she earned for using "the old-fashioned political trick of buying votes with tax dollars," Ella maintained a substantial lead over Sarasin. She hired David Garth who had been instrumental in the victories of New York mayor, Ed Koch and President Jimmy Carter, as her campaign media consultant. On television and radio, Garth promoted Mrs. Grasso as an energetic, active governor, using the slogan: "Connecticut works better because Ella works harder." In addition, Ella benefited from the continued national coverage of her candidacy in *Time, Newsweek* and other publications.

Ella's well-rehearsed theatrics also gave her an advantage over her opponent. At campaign events where Mrs. Grasso appeared together with Ronald Sarasin, she treated him arrogantly. Like her teacher, John Bailey, she acquired the ability to dismiss her challengers with merely a look. This proved particularly effective on the pre-election television debates. Several times she greeted Sarasin's comments with subtle sarcasm, lifting her eyebrows in "queenly disdain," rather than stooping to answer verbally. Observers said she did this so well that viewers seemed to take her side. Her haughty treatment of Sarasin made him appear inexperienced.

Sarasin, frustrated by Mrs. Grasso's advantages as an incumbent, a national media figure and an experienced politician, made several blatantly sexist slurs. Most notable were his references to her as "my governess." Sexism remained an issue as it had in the previous gubernatorial race. The issue of ethnicity also emerged when Lillian Carter, the President's mother, maligned Mrs. Grasso in an ethnic slur:

> Before I met Ella, I thought she was going to be a great big,
> fat woman, kind of a sweaty thing.

Mother Ella remained publicly unruffled. She refused to answer such remarks thereby separating herself from her opponent who had been reduced to name-calling and personal attacks. To her friends and staff she rarely expressed a lack of confidence or uncertainty about her re-election. It was only in the private moments she spent with her family when the ballots were being counted that she would show her insecurity. As had been her custom, Ella gathered her brood around her just before the polls closed and the returns began to be televised. She told them, in her most maternal tone, that they must be brave no matter what might happen.

Mother Ella, as many had predicted, prevailed once more. The citizens of Connecticut, over half of them from ethnic backgrounds, chose to elect an Italian-American woman governor for a second time. They did so by a huge plurality. Ella Grasso defeated Ronald Sarasin by 189,000 votes, 14,000 less than she had won in 1974; she swept in the entire state ticket and five Democratic Congress members. Her victory in 1978, however, was perhaps more impressive than that of 1974. After rating alarmingly low in the professional polls only a year before, Ella had managed, in the span of several months, to rebuild her broad bases of support and regain her electoral momentum. Mrs. Grasso's second stunning victory stood as a monument not only to her political shrewdness, but also to her immense personal power.

Chapter Eleven

HORSES THAT FLY
1979-1981

*"Six months is a long time. In six
months the horse may die, the king may
die, or the horse may learn to fly."*

Ella Grasso on state taxes.

At the opening of the 1979 legislative session, Ella began what Bailey had liked to call "a new ball game." The large plurality she had received in the 1978 gubernatorial race gave her hope for a winning season. She now had a strong mandate for continued fiscal austerity and reform. She could count on support from Democratic legislators who owed their seats to her stunning electoral success and who formed sizeable majorities in both Houses. The party, moreover, had chosen a team of legislative leaders who were loyal and devoted to her. Ernest Abate, a young Stamford legislator whom Ella had taken under her wing, replaced James Kennelly, who had been directly opposed to the governor's economic and tax policies. John Groppo, a stone mason from Winsted and a stalwart supporter of the governor, succeeded Billy O'Neill as House Majority leader. On the Senate side, Joseph Lieberman, who, during his college years at Yale, wrote a biography of John Bailey, took over as Majority leader, while Joseph Fauliso, one of Ella's closest personal friends, continued to preside as President Pro Tempore of the Senate.

Not only did Ella have control of the Legislature, but ever since the replacement of State Chairman Billy O'Neill, by John Dempsey, Jr., son of the former governor, she ruled the Democratic Party. The young Dempsey, who had worked in her Congressional office and managed her gubernatorial campaign, was devoted to her and did her bidding. As insider Jack Zaiman commented:

> ...Dempsey is her man, totally. Nothing goes by Democratic State headquarters without Grasso knowing about it, clearing it or quashing it.

Because the governor had command of both the legislative and party forces, the 1979 session ran smoothly: Mrs. Grasso got almost everything she wanted. Her Legislature adopted a budget package that surpassed her proposal by only .4%. The 5.5% increase in the General Fund was one of the lowest among all the states. The 85.4 million dollar capital program was the lowest in the state in five years. Following Ella's orders, the General Assembly coped with stagnating economic times by imposing no new taxes and by remedying, on an incremental basis, state funding inequities in education grants to local school systems. Her efforts to foster fiscal austerity brought her a fourth consecutive surplus of 66.7 million dollars.

Mrs. Grasso's General Assembly also adopted much of her agenda for return and increased social services. After three sessions of trying, she finally was successful in getting her gambling reform bill passed which would restrict state gaming operations for efficiency and would provide greater protection of the public. It reduced the speed limit to 55 miles-per-hour to help conserve gasoline and reduce accidents. Her Urban Action program, accepted by the Legislature, would direct 12 million dollars in capital funding to the needs of impoverished areas in population centers including housing, mass transit, economic development, day care, recreation, and elderly and community centers. And they poured additional dollars into innovative job training programs. When the session ended in June, the governor emerged triumphant; she had begun to reach the pinnacle of her political career.

As the summer and fall of 1979 passed, Mrs. Grasso's power and influence continued to rise considerably. In early May, Abe Ribicoff announced to the press that he would not seek a fourth term in the United States Senate. Ribicoff's retirement represented the loss of one of the state's most influential political leaders. Although Ella could not inherit Abe's clout on Capitol Hill, she did assume his stature as Connecticut's foremost political force.

The *Courant's* political writer, Jack Zaiman, commented that Ella was becoming the "Boss" of Connecticut, and as he noted, she did not appear to have any challengers. During July, Ella moved to strengthen her influence in both the state and national spheres.

She shrewdly seized the opportunity to enhance her image among her constituents by acting as a crisis manager during the period of gasoline shortages that summer. She quickly set up an equitable system of odd-even gasoline rationing to ease hoarding and long lines at gas stations. She also opened an emergency gasoline center at the State Armory. Reporters roamed the headquarters there while she responded to the requests of constituents and gave orders to her staff. Mother Ella answered some of these calls to the center herself. The press reported that:

> She [Grasso] spent an afternoon pushing her glasses from the bridge of her nose to the top of head, taking notes and murmuring words of encouragement to callers.

In her customary style, Mrs. Grasso went through several largely symbolic motions to dramatize alternative solutions to the energy crisis. She used her Honda car, which got fifty miles per gallon, and on weekends she took the train to her cottage on the Connecticut shore.

Ella also enhanced her national image during the crisis. Unanimously elected as Chairperson of the Northeastern coalition of governors, she helped organize those states to act in the interest of achieving equitable pricing and distribution of oil. She took a highly publicized trip to Washington to discuss Connecticut's plight with President Carter and Energy Secretary Schlesinger. She was part of the first group of governors called to Camp David to talk about energy issues with the President.

When Carter's campaign for the presidential nomination got under way, party leaders and political writers began to mention Governor Grasso as a possible running mate, along with other Northeastern Democrats including New York Senator Daniel Patrick Moynihan, New Jersey Governor Brendan Byrne, and New York Governor Hugh Carey. Mrs. Grasso's supporters argued that her Catholicism and ethnic identification would strengthen Carter's candidacy in the Northeast. As in the 1976 campaign, Ella Grasso was also mentioned as a potential presidential candidate. Saunders Kahn, a New York economist, began a one-man campaign to promote Governor Grasso for President. Ella responded evasively to subsequent queries about her political ambitions by saying enigmatically: "I will grow where I am planted."

In Connecticut, Ella Grasso showed the substance of her leadership and the strength of her political style one terrifying afternoon early in October when a tornado struck the towns of Windsor, Windsor Locks, and Suffield. The governor, now an experienced crisis manager, surveyed the devastated areas and then asked President Carter to declare a major disaster and to obtain federal aid. Within a few days she had secured temporary housing structures for those left homeless by the storm. The governor herself supervised the distribution and delivery of the mobile homes Carter sent to Connecticut.

As in the blizzard of 1978, Mrs. Grasso's superb handling of the press further enhanced her image. Reporters followed her when she toured badly damaged residential areas and talked to local officials. They watched their governor tramp around in the mud and wreckage wearing work clothes and a baseball cap pulled down over a bandanna as she commanded the clean-up operations. And when a policewoman in Windsor Locks told Ella that newspeople were trying to travel on the debris-clogged Route 75 to see the hardest hit areas, the governor ordered the officer to "let those reporters through."

While playing the role of the efficient state manager, Mrs. Grasso also revealed her compassionate side during the crisis. She gave consolation and comfort to victims of the tornado. When she saw an old woman who had lost her property standing outside shivering in the cold, she gave the woman the heavy sweater she was wearing. The governor personally delivered six large boxes of sandwiches to hungry workers in the emergency headquarters at the Poquonock fire station in Windsor. She also delivered a message for a distraught mother in North Carolina who had heard that the tornado had struck in Windsor Locks where her son was living. Her son promptly received a chiding call from the governor who told him "Call your mother—she's worried sick." Mother Ella again endeared herself to her electorate.

Shortly afterwards, Mrs. Grasso responded successfully to another crisis—the energy crisis exacerbated by the supply policies of the OPEC countries. With winter approaching and oil prices rising to higher and higher levels, the governor worried that the state's poor and aged could not survive the cold. Demonstrating the "decisiveness of a true leader," Ella called the General Assembly into a special session. Together the governor and the Legislature worked productively to create a multi-million dollar aid package that would assure the neediest families of heat as well as provide economic incentives for all state residents to conserve energy.

The special session had been a success. Yet the General Assembly had treated only the symptoms rather than the cause of the crisis. Spiraling energy prices had already begun to ravage the state's economy; many firms were leaving for warmer climates. Unemployment levels in the state, which Mrs. Grasso had managed to keep under the national average, began to rise again. Predictably, the state's budget suffered as a result of the economic downturn and the Governor again faced a revenue shortfall in the following year. She would need to increase taxes.

Some of the Democratic leaders in the Legislature urged Ella to act early to avoid the impending fiscal crisis by proposing tax hikes in the special session. Ignoring the political expediency of raising taxes in an off-election year for General Assembly members, Mrs. Grasso refused to comply. When Senator Richard Schneller, charirman of the Appropriations Committee asked her why she would not call for higher taxes, Ella answered by telling a story which ran:

> In my family we have a story about a king. One day this king got angry at his chief advisor because he gave him

125

some bad advice. As a punishment, the king ordered the advisor to teach his royal horse to fly. If the advisor did not succeed in six months, he would be sentenced to death. Members of the court asked the advisor if he was worried about teaching the horse to fly. The advisor answered that he was not, for he said: "Six months is a long time. In six months the horse may die, the king may die, I may die or the horse may learn to fly."

The story captured the essence of Ella's long-range planning; it clearly illustrated Mrs. Grasso's desire to avoid making decisions that were potentially unpopular for as long as possible, because as Bailey often pointed out, the situation might change and make the unpopular action unnecessary. Ella's decision to put off a plea for higher taxes in 1979 proved consistent with her past handling of the state's fiscal problems. In the early part of her first administration, she had refused to make priority decisions about spending cuts; she successfully side-stepped inevitable conflicts between interest groups by imposing across-the-board cuts. The governor's inaction in the area of budgetary priority-setting had been rewarded in her second year as governor when the economy improved and a surplus accrued, making it unnecessary for her to revamp the state's spending structure immediately. In that case, the horse had flown as she had hoped.

By the opening of the 1980 session, however, the horse did not appear to know how to fly. Energy prices and unemployment levels in the state continued to rise. The governor's advisors predicted a revenue gap of over 128 million dollars. Ella had no choice but to call for a one and one-half percent increase in the sales tax to seven and one-half percent as well as for a 63.3 million dollar increase in other taxes. Because she enjoyed tight control over her party's forces in the legislature, tax increases were accomplished with a "minimum of contentiousness," despite the impending elections for General Assembly members that fall. The Assembly approved a one-half percent increase in the sales tax and passed a two percent tax on the gross earnings of the state's major oil companies.

Because Ella could still balance the budget by increasing taxes despite the difficult economic times, she avoided serious consideration of an income tax as a remedy for the state's economic ills. Consistent with her flying horse philosophy, she continued to "wait and see", putting aside the income tax issue. She could manage the state's fiscal affairs without a revised revenue structure for a few more years. As long as the possibility of keeping the state solvent without the unpopular tax remained real, the governor would refuse to speak of its possible future necessity to the public or urge the Legislature to take up the study of its potential impact.

The governor attempted to meet the challenge of maintaining existing levels of state services in the face of economic decline by vigorously promoting economic development. A healthy state economy meant more jobs, more spending, and more revenue. She worked closely with Ed Stockton of the state's department of Economic Development to attract overseas firms to Connecticut. By the end of fiscal 1980, new firms from Germany, Sweden, Switzerland, Scotland, Canada, Belgium, and Japan had located operations in the state as result of Stockton's efforts. Incentives offered in the form of tax breaks and job training programs continued to draw other companies to the state as well as to encourage existing firms to expand their current operations in Connecticut.

In March of 1980, as Governor Grasso began to work with the General Assembly to avert the projected budget deficit, problems with her health developed. Early in the month, she experienced bleeding and pain while at her vacation home in Old Lyme. She was admitted to Hartford Hospital for dilation and curettage, then discharged. Examination of the tissue removed during the procedure, however, contained malignant cells. She was readmitted to Hartford Hospital where exploratory surgery revealed an ovarian mass which was removed by her doctor, Joseph N. Russo. As the extent of the tumor was uncertain, Russo also performed a hysterectomy at the same time. Two weeks later, Russo revealed to the press that in fact an ovarian cancer had been removed during surgery.

When newspapers revealed the nature of Ella's illness after the operation had been performed, many people in the state expressed grave concern. On April 19, the governor held a press conference with

Russo to discuss her condition. At that time Russo pronounced the operation "completely successful"; he predicted that her life expectancy "would not be altered in any way." Tests showed that all the cancer cells had been removed and the possibility of recurrence, Russo said, was minimal. As a preventative measure, however, he prescribed several weeks of chemotherapy. Russo's report and Mrs. Grasso's optimism at the conference reassured her people.

Soon after the surgery, Mrs. Grasso resumed much of her demanding schedule. She postponed the chemotherapy until the day after the Legislature closed, so she could work fully on her agenda for the remainder of the session. When Ella did begin treatment on May 8, she reacted badly to it. For two months she suffered from the debilitating side effects of the chemotherapy. She couldn't eat. She was constantly tired. She endured nausea and diarrhea. Her staff, her friends, and her collagues could not help but notice her discomfort.

Still, Ella remained actively involved in the presidential campaign. She worked hard for her friend, President Jimmy Carter. In August, she presided as Chair of the Credentials Committee at the Democratic National Convention held at Madison Square Garden. Noticeably thinner, drawn, and pale, Ella nonetheless attended every session of the committee meetings and stood proudly beside President Carter when he called her to the podium after he received the Democratic nomination.

After the convention, Ella continued to suffer from the side effects of the recent chemotherapy treatments. She continued to lose weight. The doctors diagnosed gastritis, an inflammation of the stomach lining. A diet of soft foods did little to alleviate her symptoms. Russo attributed her gastric problems to the pressures of the Presidential campaign, her inhuman schedule, and her tendency to keep her emotions to herself. Always a tough taskmaster both on her staff and herself, Ella insisted on attending not only to her duties as governor but also to her party political obligations. She displayed an unemotional exterior, refusing to show her feelings or to confide in her friends.

Throughout the fall of 1980, her condition did not improve. Rumors that she would resign began to surface. On November 17, only ten days after Carter's defeat, she entered Hartford Hospital for treatment of an inflamed vein in her leg. Shortly after her bout with phlebitis, doctors diagnosed what many had feared since April—that cancer had spread to her liver. Though she had little reason to be optimistic, for most victims of metastatic ovarian cancer did not live more than a year after diagnosis, the stoic Mrs. Grasso then ran the state from her hospital room, as Bailey had commanded the Party after throat cancer confined him to his bed. At her sickest, she made twenty telephone calls a day, read the state newspapers, signed letters and bills, and complained that her staff did not bring her enough work.

Seeking solace during this difficult time, Ella would return to her home in Old Lyme almost every weekend. The press corps, curious about her health, the grueling presidential campaign, and the crowded legislative session made her official duties physically and emotionally draining. She needed the hours alone to rest and rejuvenate. She took long walks with Tom and stitched her needlepoint Christmas projects. Susanne and Jimmy, began to spend more of their weekends in Old Lyme with their mother.

Ella, an intensely proud woman, had but one alternative. She had to leave her office while she could still "hold her head high." On Decmber 1, she walked out of the hospital without prior notice. Two days later, her political assistant, Chad McCollam, made a round of calls to the Democratic Legislative leadership. "She's going to pull the plug on herself," he told Speaker of the House Ernie Abate. The next morning, on Decemeber 4 at 8 a.m., Speaker Abate, President Pro Tempore Fauliso, Leiutenant Governor O'Neill, Majority Leader Groppo, and State Chairman Fitzgerald gathered at the residence for a meeting with Governor Grasso. Ella told them that because she could no longer give her full energy to her office, she would be leaving the Governor's Office at the end of the working day on December 31st. After presenting each with a brass memento with her likeness on it, she kissed them and told them to "come by and see" her. They were all in tears. Ella did not cry.

Later that morning, she gave a written and a tape-recorded statement of her resignation to the press. Her brief message read:

> Regretfully, it is my belief that I do not have the stamina
> or the endurance for the rigors of the new legislative session

and the myriad of problems that face the administration of a vital and vibrant state.

All of my life has been one of dedication to working for people. I ask God's help that I may continue to do so. I thank again the many who have sent me prayers and good wishes. I love you. I love you all.

On December eighth, Ella returned to Hartford Hospital for a colostomy and more chemotherapy. Her condition deteriorated as the cancer spread to her large and small intestines. Despite her weakness, Ella did not forget her favorite holiday. She enlisted the staff at the residence to finish her final preparations, for most of the shopping and wrapping she had done herself several months before. The state troopers who had driven her to official engagements received elaborate delivery instructions. Ella requested that the troopers ask the recipients to open the gift in their presence so she could get a second-hand account of the individual's reaction. Aware of her condition, all of her friends who received a gift that year were deeply moved.

When Bill O'Neill was sworn in as governor and Joseph Fauliso took the oath as Lieutenant Governor at the end of the day on December thirty-first, Ella lay in guarded condition. Two weeks later, her doctors down-graded her condition to "serious." During this time, she never lost consciousness. On the first day of February, however, she slid into a semi-comatose state. Four days later, on February fifth, at 6:03 p.m., Ella Grasso died at Hartford Hospital.

Shortly after her death, her body was brought to the Capitol rotunda where she lay in state just a few feet from what had been her office when she was Secretary of State. Over 5,000 people braved the heavy rain to file past her coffin. On the morning of February ninth, her funeral was held at St. Josph's Cathedral in Hartford. All the living former governors, members of the state's congressional delegation, Secretary of State Alexander Haig, the state Supreme Court justices, as well as party leaders, politicians, friends and relatives went to the Cathedral to honor Ella Grasso.

To her people she was Mother Ella. Departing from tradition, her son Jim delivered the simple and moving eulogy heard on radio and television across the state:

> She gave to all of you what she gave to my sister, Susanne, and me...a mother's gift of unselfish love, understanding, compassion and tenderness...

.   .   .

> In closing, I would like to share with you a few phrases from a letter written by my mother some time ago in which she expressed a desire to have mentioned at her funeral the following:

> In my house there is a motto which says, "Bloom where you are planted." That is Windsor Locks which is my strength and my life.

After the funeral, her body was taken home to Windsor Locks. Mothers with babies in their arms, school children, and servicemen lined up in silence along the streets as the 115-car cortege made its way through the town toward St. Mary's Church. That afternoon Ella was buried beside her parents, Maria and Giacomo Tambussi, at St. Mary's Cemetary.

Epilogue

IN GRANITE OR IN CLAY?

The myth of Mother Ella survived intact for nearly two years after she left office. After her tragic death, everyone remembered her fondly; some of her fiercest enemies spoke glowingly of her. School buildings, a street, and a highway were named for her. Committees formed to raise money for a statue in her likeness. A scholarship for deserving college students and an award for outstanding Connecticut women in public service were established in her memory.

During this time, few articles appeared that criticized Mrs. Grasso or her administration, except for what some called a "bitter" portrayal written by Gail Collins and published by the *Advocate* one year after her death. Connecticut readers, however, had come to expect nothing more and nothing less from the *Advocate*, which had routinely printed sharp and sometimes harsh critiques of Grasso's administration. Even when Arthur Powers, her former campaign manager and prime fund-raiser, whom she appointed Commissioner of the Transportation Department (the state's largest agency), underwent investigation by a one-man grand jury for charges of bid-rigging and other irregularities in 1982, Ella's reputation remained unblemished. Powers stood trial for taking bribes from architecture and construction firms, many of whom had made large contributions to Grasso's campaigns, and for awarding contracts to these firms over lower bidders. But the myth of Mother Ella persisted: car bumpers still bore green and white "Thank you Ella" that Powers himself had paid for and distributed shortly before she died.

In early 1983, however, the myth suffered its first scathing attack. On January 9, the *Hartford Courant*, whose reporters she had coddled and "cowed," published an article written by Robert Satter, a Superior Court judge, in its Sunday "Northeast Magazine," which criticized not only Mother Ella but also her mentors, Abe Ribicoff and John Bailey. In his article about the political legacy left by those three figures— figures he called so popular among the electorate that the "Connecticut version of Mount Rushmore" would feature their carved heads—the judge attacked the three monuments in Connecticut politics for gain- ing their immense personal power by avoiding divisive issues. As governors, Grasso and Ribicoff, he argued, "knew their issues and potential solutions better than the public and yet they let the public limit their performance in office." Because they were not willing to sacrifice votes in order to educate the public about the personal income tax, or other possible longterm solutions to the state's financial ills, the former state legislator concluded that Grasso and her mentors "mired government in mediocrity" and for that reason the likenesses of three Connecticut heroes should be carved "not in granite but in clay."

In his analysis, Satter argued strenuously that Ella Grasso practiced the "politics of avoidance" and linked this aspect of her leadership style to her tutelage under Bailey and Ribicoff. Ella's leadership style, however, can be traced not only to her training with the chairman, but also to her experiences in the community where she grew up, in her years at Mount Holyoke, and in Windsor Locks town politics. But other influences which shaped the political styles of populist and machine politicians like Al Smith and Fiorello LaGuardia were present in Ella's formative years. Her background gave use to two distinct impulses which have been described as "managerial" and "populistic" characteristics.

Like the politicians who have been characterized as managers such as Hoover and Eisenhower, Ella Grasso grew up in a family that was neither poor nor privileged. She was a member of the rising middle class and did not know poverty or the slums. She was the child of immigrants living in an ethnic neighborhood, so she knew about the cares and concerns of Connecticut's ethnic residents, the majority of the state's population. She shared the state's dominant religion, Catholicism; and she spoke the language of the dominant ethnic group, Italian. A daughter of parents who once labored in town factories, she knew intimately of the struggle of the state's blue collar workers and could communicate easily and effectively with them using her rather folksy speech.

Ella made effective use of an unpretentious style that emphasized her stance among working people. Rather than embrace the trappings of executive office, Ella deliberately shunned some of them in order to make it clear that it was service and not status that interested her. She refused to use the gubernatorial limosine and chose instead to travel around the state in an economy car. Her clothing remained decidedly frumpy. At the "governor's mansion," which she began calling the "governor's residence" because it sounded less pompous, she served lasagna instead of the expected duck l'orange when her friends of the Windsor Locks Democratic Town Committee came to dinner there.

Ella Grasso learned early that she had a stake in the system. Like her counterparts in the Boston and New York machines, she took up the political trades by apprenticing herself first to the local Democratic Party organization under Rabbett and Fitzpatrick and then to the state organization run by Boss Bailey. Under their tutelage, she developed her skill in the use of power. She knew when to amass it and when to expend it. She accumulated political capital by focusing on relatively non-controversial issues to avoid alienating her people. She did not take strong steps in the more controversial areas of urban affairs, public utility regulation, and the tax structure. Instead, she centered her agenda on a balanced budget, consumer protection, freedom of information, and elderly rights. By accumulating large surpluses and increasing her support across party lines through legislation relating to consumers, senior citizens, and access to public information, Ella Grasso insured the success of her agenda as well as her reelection in '78.

Managerial elements in Grasso's background also shaped Ella's gubernatorial agenda. Her upbringing in the frugal household of a rising middle-class shopkeeper, her economics training at Mount Holyoke, her small-town belief in private enterprise, and her early attraction to the Republican Party, all underlay her advocacy of government reorganization. As chief executive, the long-time apostle of efficiency in government, pressed successfully for complete reorganiztion of the state's bureaucracy, streamlining its 200 offices into 22 superagencies.

Other managerial impulses surfaced in her very pragmatic and un-ideological attitude toward campaign issues and public policy. In her election campaigns, Ella ran on what is considered by many to be managerial platform, promising to clean up corruption in gaming, to reform the state civil service, and to eliminate waste in government spending. Her campaign appeals stressed her successful management of the state's economy; she emphasized that she had done a "good job," leading her consultant David Garth to create the slogan: "Connecticut works better because Ella works harder."

Another element in her style which may be characterized as "maternal," emerged from the family-centered Italian-American culture dominated by women. It is this element which distinguished her from her male predecessors in Conecticut politics. Ella gained the confidence of many individuals who witnessed her maternal caring and compassion. She paid the insurance premium of a state worker who needed financial help. She wrote letters of comfort to bereaved families. When poverty-stricken constituents came to the office hours she held regularly, she often gave them money for food. In the winter of 1978, when the blizzard paralyzed Connecticut, she mothered the entire state, offering frequent words of encouragement over television and radio.

Although the populist, the managerial, and the maternal elements in her executive style contributed to Governor Grasso's electoral and political success, they did limit her capacity for active government. Ella's training under Bailey, as Judge Satter argued, kept her from moving toward long-term solutions to the state's most pressing problems. To Grasso, like Bailey, winning mattered most. Issues came second. She correctly identified issues important to her constituency, but she did not view them as policy imperatives once in office. Throughout her first campaign for governor, Ella promised to create a new Public Utilities Authority which would give citizens a strong voice in the rate-making process. This issue, which was particularly timely given the litigation against the utilities that year, brought widespread support. After her victory in November, however, Mrs. Grasso did not work actively for a strong PUCA. Her weak appointments to that board further disappointed those who had backed the governor initially. Likewise, in the beginning months of the campaign, she promised property tax reform in order to gain the votes of those in the Hartford area for the primary against Killian. After that race, in which she trounced Killian, she quickly abandoned her pledge to overhaul the tax system even before her fight for the governorship had ended, for she did not want to risk alienating those in suburban areas. In both of her gubernatorial campaigns, she staunchly opposed the personal income tax, as had Ribbicoff and Bailey, who both considered its political consequences to be disastrous. Similarly, even after her reelection to the governorship, she refused to sacrifice her great popularity to educate the public about the need to restructure Connecticut's crumbling tax system. On other issues, she expressed strong dissatisfaction with existing conditions in the areas of urban affairs and public utility regulation, but she never took strong steps to correct what she perceived as problems for fear of losing her political support.

Ella's application of managerial tactics to fiscal problems also usually resulted in the creation of short-run solutions to the state's economic ills. She balanced budgets without a guiding philosophy. Often accused of being a line-item budgeter, she cut where she could avoid incurring the wrath of agencies and interest groups. The governor, who had a rather stormy relationship with her Legislature, especially during her first term, sought purely administrative solutions to the state's revenue problems. She made across-the-board cuts in department spending to avoid the difficult process of reordering spending priorities.

Finally Mrs. Grasso's maternal style worked in the same direction, making her administration merely a preservation of the status quo. Mrs. Grasso spent long hours visiting the sick, writing notes of sympathy, expressing concern in individual cases. Governors must perform such symbolic tasks, but Ella Grasso, shrewdly aware of the political implications of these acts, spent perhaps too much time at these tasks which kept her away from other policy-making activities. Often described as a "friend of the poor," she consistently refused to change the state's income structure to relieve the burden of the state's high sales tax that bore most heavily on the poor. Her well-publicized mothering, however, appeared to convince those that might have been skeptical about her true compassion or her commitment to the idea that the state should serve the people.

Governor Grasso's unique political style made her immensely popular at the polls. During her three decades of public life, she never lost an election. As Secretary of State, she had led the Democratic ticket, capturing thousands more votes than the successful incumbent governor, Abraham Ribicoff. Unharmed by the Republican landslide in 1972, she won her Congressional seat by almost 50,000 votes. And in her second gubernatorial race, she polled more votes than had any other candidate to that office to date.

When Ella Grasso was first elected to the governorship in 1974, feminists and liberals rejoiced. They held high hopes that her administration would be substantively different than those of her male predecessors. Her refusals to support a pro-choice policy and other women's issues alienated these supporters. She pursued "politics as usual" and made no major changes in the state's fiscal policy or its revenue structure, leading many to compare her administration with the previous Republican governor, Thomas Meskill.

Indeed, Ella's performance in office did not distinguish her from her male counterparts. It was rather her unique political style that set her apart. The Mother Ella image she cultivated certainly did not have an analogue among male politicians, for it had arisen out her experience as a woman. She shrewdly used her femininity, most notably by expressing her caring and concern for individuals in ways that men could not. She hugged the physically handicapped, comforted the homeless, and kissed the aged.

Yet the maternal element in Governor Grasso's political style did not move her toward the type of active, progressive leadership the public had looked forward to. Aware of its benefits on election day, Ella used this style only to enhance her public image and to gain votes. She did not, however, use this successful personal style, as Franklin D. Roosevelt and other dynamic leaders had, to win support for innovative fiscal and legislative agendas. She refused to exploit the tactics she employed in accumulating political capital to promote her policies, leaving her gubernatorial record undistinguishable from her male predecessors. Consequently, the maternal element of her political character— the compassionate and concerned Mother Ella image that had brought her unparalleled success at the polls—made her, in the end, a caretaker rather than a crusader in state government.

The answer to the question of why Ella did not use the popularity she so carefully cultivated, lies perhaps in her roots in Windsor Locks. As a day student at an exclusive boarding school and later as a scholarship student at an elite private college, she had lived as an outsider in two vastly different worlds—the working class ethnic community where she was raised and the wealthy upper middle class circles in which she was educated. Her education ultimately separated her from the former while her ethnic background precluded her from full assimilation into the latter. In politics Ella found the complete acceptance she had lacked in her earlier life. Ella's shrewd accumulation of political capital and her conscious development of her unique style brought her unparalleled success at the polls. As Mother Ella she thrived both personally and politically. Her electorate willingly exchanged their votes for her maternal presence. It was a mutual affection.

NOTES

Ella Grasso was the first woman governor who was not preceded in the post by her husband. Nellie Ross was elected governor of Wyoming in 1925, the same year that Miriam "Ma" Ferguson was elected governor of Texas, but both women came to office on the coattails of their husbands. Ferguson, however, was reelected in 1933 after she had established her own political identity. In 1967, the state of Alabama elected Lurleen Wallace as governor to succeed her husband. In 1976, two years after Ella was elected governor of Connecticut, Dixie Lee Ray became governor of Washington. In 1983, Kentucky elected Martha Layne Collins as governor.

PREFACE

1. Moira Lyons is the first ... : Center for American Women and Politics *Fact Sheet,* 2001.
2. Although Connecticut is a national example ... Center for American Women and Politics *Fact Sheet,* 2001.

CHAPTER 3

1. A former enthusiast of FDR ...: Sylvio Preli to SB, interview, 30 Aug. 1982.

CHAPTER 4

1. Though flexible and progressive ...: Alexander Goldfarb to SB, interview 22 June 1982.

2. In a matter of months ...: *Hartford Courant* (hereinafter "Courant"), 7 Aug. 1956.

3. Sound and practical political thinker ...: Joseph Lieberman, *The Legacy,* (Spoonwood Press, 1982), p. 53.

4. Good candidate, good issues ...: *Courant,* 16 Sept. 1952.

5. Let the candidate's personality ...: *Legacy,* p. 53.

6. lore of Connecticut politics ...: *Ibid.*

7. Whether the American dream is still alive ...: *Ibid*, p. 54.

8. Your father was a man ...: Preli to SB, 30 Aug. 1982.

9. How she runs a household, *Courant*, 7 May 1955.

CHAPTER 5

1. The secretaryship offered ...: Gloria Schaffer to SB, 12 Sept. 1982.

2. John Bailey was like ...: Robert Satter to SB

3. More than a nice housewife ...: William Ratchford to SB, 19 Aug. 1982.

4. Ella considered Dempsey to be ...: Schaffer to SB, 12 Sept. 1982.

5. Dempsey had to tolerate ...: Leo Donahue to SB, 17 July 1982.

6. disagreements over large and small ...: Amalia Toro to SB, 17 Sept. 1982.

7. Strong-willed women ...: Schaffer to SB, 12 Sept. 1982.

8. The chair will take ...: *Courant*, 22 Aug. 1964.

9. the pillar of party power ...: *Legacy*, p. 118.

10. Madame Secretary still had time ...: *Courant* 3 July 1966.

11. His traditional notions ...: Schaffer, 12 Sept. 1982.

CHAPTER 6

1. It is a panel that has listened ...: Courant, 31 Jan. 1971.

2. Travel on the inside track ...: *New Haven Advocate*, 18 March 1981.

3. I can be a gadfly ...: Susan and Martin Tolchin, *Clout: Womanpower and Politics* (Coward, McCann and Goegan, Inc., 1973) p. 90.

4. Not proven herself to be a 'superwoman' ...: Jarin and Burkhart, *Ella Grasso: Democratic Representative from Connecticut*, Ralph Nader Congress Project, 1972), p. 25.

CHAPTER 7

1. Whadd'ya hear about ...: Larry Cacciola to SB, 21 July 1982.

2. Carbone and his allies ...: Nicholas Carbone to SB, 24 July 1982.

3. big money & the old politics ...: *Valley Advocate,* 10 Oct. 1974.

4. If she gets the job ...: *Connecticut Magazine,* May/June 1974, p. 26.

5. She's not what you'd call ...: "Running & Winning," *Ms.,* Oct. 1974, p. 81.

6. I would like to think that I ...: *Connecticut Magazine,* June 1974, p. 26.

7. People aren't looking at me, *Valley Advocate,* 10 Oct. 1974, p. 4.

8. I see it as a people's job ...: *Connecticut Magazine,* June 1974, p. 26.

9. forget the issues ...: *Legacy,* p. 53.

10. Whadd'ya gonna do ...: Marilyn Seictar to SB, 17 Sept. 1982.

11. Both her parents were grammar ...: *Time,* 18 November 1974.

12. A Phi Beta Kappa ...: *Time,* 29 July 1974, p. 28.

13. hand-picked by her boss ...: *Legacy,* p. 196.

14. How can you say you're against ...: Duane Lockard, *New England State Politics* (Princeton: Princeton University Press, 1959), p. 262.

CHAPTER 8

1. Leirnsohn would be the undisputed boss ...: Ken Alwetta, "Mother Ella," *Connecticut Magazine,* June, 1975, p. 22.

2. A workingman's diner in front ...: *New Haven Register,* 9 January 1975.

3. The situation is serious ...: "Inaugural Message to the General Assembly," Journal of the House, 8 January 1975.

4. Her critics agreed that she ...: *Connecticut Magazine,* June 1975, p. 25.

5. Bella Abzug, chided Ella ...: *Courant,* 26 Aug. 1975.

6. A woman who could become ...: *Courant* 21 Sept. 1975.

CHAPTER 9

1. robbing the veteran's piggy bank …: *Hartford Advocate*, 25 Feb. 1976, p. 6.

2. hate what the veterans hate …: *Ibid.*

3. sleazy tactics …: *Connecticut Magazine*, Sept. 1976, p. 14.

4. a buidget of cream puffs …: *Ibid.*

5. lusting after an income tax …: Jay Tepper to SB, 18 July 1982.

6. budget of gimmicks …: *Connecticut Magazine*, Sept. 1976.

7. cheapos and attempted to form a new political coalition …: *Hartford Advocate*, 23 March 1977, p. 6.

CHAPTER 10

1. trying his damdest to look important …: Ronald Sarasin to SB, 17 Aug. 1982.

2. OK, is he here? …: *Ibid.*

3. Mother Ella …: *Connecticut Magazine*, June 1975, p. 22.

4. compassionate, strong … maternal …: *Legacy*, p. 205.

5. What male candidate, even if he could …: *Courant*, n.d., p. 4, Joel Lang, "A Governor's Retrospective."

6. But you're all my children …: Michael Riley to SB, 4 Aug. 1982.

7. Well, h-e-l-l-o-o-o, children …: Nancy Lewinsohm to SB, 8 June 1982.

8. Don't worry, mother is here …: Michael Riley to SB.

9. If reports wanted to know about the budget …: *Hartford Advocate*, 18 March 1981.

10. have you met Gail Collins? …: John Groppo to SB, 4 Aug. 1982.

11. Why the SOB wrote that …: Edward Stockton to SB, 22 June 1982.

12. brutal, foul-mouthed, and bitchy …: Sarasin to SB.

13. Before I met Ella …: *Courant*, 13 Oct. 1978.

CHAPTER 11

1. Dempsey is her man …: *Courant*, 6 May 1979.

2. She spent an afternoon pushing up …: *Courant*, 22 July 1979.

3. I will grow where I am planted …: *Courant*, 12 Aug. 1979.

4. let those reporters through …: *Courant*, 8 Oct. 1979.

5. Call your mother …: *Ibid.*

6. In my family we have a story …: Gardner Wright to SB,

7. Regretfully, it is my belief …: *Courant*, 5 Dec. 1980.